Caxton's Printing Office in the Almonry at Westminster.

(From the picture by Daniel Maclise, R.A.)

1. Earl Rivers, Caxton's patron. 2. The Abbot of Westminster. 3. Duke of Clarence. 4. Queen of Edward the Fourth. 5. King Edward the Fourth. 6. Richard of Gloucester, slain at Bosworth 1485. 7. William Caxton, died 1491. 8. Princess Elizabeth of York. 9. The young Princes, murdered in the Tower 1483. 10. Compositors and Pressmen. 11. Bookbinders, Wood Engravers, Illuminators.

THE ROYAL SCHOOL SERIES

Highroads of History

*Illustrated by the great Historical Paintings of
John Pettie, Daniel Maclise, Thomas Stothard, C. W. Cope,
William Dyce, B. W. Leader, W. Bell Scott,
Sir E. J. Poynter, Sir John Gilbert,
W. F. Yeames, Edward Armitage,
Ford Madox Brown, &c.*

Other Days and Other Ways

(From the Earliest Times to 1485)

THOMAS NELSON AND SONS

London, Edinburgh, Dublin, and New York

1907

CONTENTS.

Other Days and Other Ways.

I. STONEHENGE.—I.

1. Come with me to Wiltshire, where there is a wide stretch of rolling downs known as Salisbury Plain. All round it are chalk hills, broad white roads cross it, and small rivers cut their way through it. In the valleys are quiet hamlets nestling amidst trees, and around them are smiling cornfields and broad meadows.

2. The Plain itself is unfit for tillage. No plough turns up its chalky surface, for the soil is thin and poor. A short, springy turf covers it, and on this sheep browse in thousands. Formerly it was remote and solitary, a place of loneliness and silence broken only by the cry of the peewit, the bleat of the sheep, or the bark of the dog. Now it is peopled with soldiers, horse, foot, and artillery; for the Government has purchased the greater part of it as a camp of exercise for our army. Throughout the summer the Plain rings with the call of bugles, the crack of rifles, and the roar of big guns.

3. The Plain is of little importance in itself, but no place in Great Britain will serve better as a starting-point for our

history lessons. Everywhere we see the remains of people who dwelt in our land many centuries ago. Scattered over the Plain are the barrows in which these old inhabitants lie buried; their fortresses and watch-towers crown the heights along its borders; their dikes, trenches, and roads are still to be seen. Here, for example, is the great stronghold known as Old Sarum, a huge mound in three terraces, which was a place of importance as far back as the days of the Romans.

4. Far older still is Stonehenge, a great monument of stone, majestic even in ruin. Look at this picture, which shows you Stonehenge as it is to-day. What you see is a collection of huge sandstone boulders, or " sarsens," gray with lichens, and worn by the storms of ages. Some of them are sixteen feet high, some are still taller. Several of the pairs of upright stones are crossed by stone slabs, and look not unlike a series of doorways.

5. At first sight the stones seem to be in no sort of order. Learned men, however, have carefully studied the plan on which they were first set up, and under their guidance we can readily form an idea of what Stonehenge looked like when it was complete. It was approached by a long avenue running from north-east to south-west, and defended on either side by ditches. This led to a circular earthwork, in the middle of which stood the real Stonehenge.

6. First, there was a huge outer circle of upstanding boulders planted side by side like door-posts, and joined at the top by cap-stones, forming a great ring of stone. Within this circle there was an inner circle of darker

coloured " blue stones ; " and within the inner circle were two horse-shoe curves, the outer and larger formed of huge " sarsens," over twenty feet high, and arranged in groups of two joined by lintels, the inner and smaller consisting of " blue stones." Both the horse-shoes face the north-east. Within the inner horse-shoe is a great slab known as the Altar Stone or Sun Stone, because the earliest rays of the rising sun on Midsummer Day fall upon it. Near at hand is another slab known as the Slaughter Stone.

STONEHENGE AS IT IS TO-DAY.

7. The first question we ask ourselves is, Why were these stones set up in this way ? No one really knows, but many people think that they formed a vast temple to the Sun god. If they are right, it was to this place, lifted high above the valley mists and open to sun and star, that the early inhabitants of our islands gathered to worship the sun, and to hold their great national meetings.

8. Some tell us that here the gray-bearded Druids, clad in spotless white and with a circlet of oak leaves upon their brows, chanted their hymns and offered up their sacrifices. These men, you will remember, were the prophets, priests,

judges, doctors, and poets of the Britons. They formed the learned class, and enjoyed great honour amongst their fellow-countrymen, who feared them greatly. It is quite possible that the Druids may have worshipped and sacrificed both animals and human beings at Stonehenge, but very probably generations of priests of quite another race worshipped in the same place long before them.

KITS COITY HOUSE (KENT).

Cromlechs of this kind are found in all parts of the British Isles, but especially in Ireland, where there are 780 of them. They are either old places of worship, or mark the burial-place of some chieftain.

9. The next question we ask ourselves is, Who built this ancient temple? Here again we can give no certain answer, though we can perhaps get a clue by examining the tools which have been dug up within the temple and in its immediate neighbourhood. All of them are made of stone ; in all the digging that has taken place round about the ruin, only one small piece of copper has been found.

10. Now, in the days of the Druids the men of Britain knew the use of copper, bronze, and iron. Stonehenge would therefore seem to have been built by men who worked only with tools of stone. Probably Stonehenge was built by people who lived in what is called the New Stone Age, some thousands of years before the birth of Christ.

2. STONEHENGE.—II.

1. Round about Stonehenge is the graveyard of the temple, with hundreds of burial-mounds or barrows. Some of these tombs are older and some are younger than the temple itself. Many of them have been opened, and have been found to contain human and other remains. From the oldest of these barrows we learn something about the Iberian, or man of the New Stone Age.

2. He was small, dark-haired, wiry, and strong, a good hunter and a good fighter. He had tamed such animals as the dog, horse, goat, sheep, cow, and pig ; he could grow corn, could spin and weave, and make earthen pots to hold water. He dug deep into the ground to find flints with which to make his stone axes, saws, and spears ; and he could draw pictures of birds and beasts on the rocks. For the most part he lived in caves or earth-houses, which were approached by a low passage, through which the members of the family had to creep in and out.

3. The next question which we ask ourselves is, How did the Iberians transport and raise the huge stones which form this vast monument ? We know that they had no

traction engines and no steam or hydraulic cranes such as
we have to-day.   Probably they worked in much the same
way as the Egyptians did when rearing their Pyramids.

4. The stones selected for the building of Stonehenge were
probably placed on rollers formed of the trimmed trunks of
trees.   Then ropes made of strips of hide were attached
to the stones, and hundreds of men slowly hauled them
across the downs to the site of the temple.   Here they
were placed in position by digging a hole in the ground
with one side sloping and the other side perpendicular.
The great stones were slipped over the slope, raised into
position with levers and ropes, and packed with rubble and
stones.

5. The raising of the lintels, however, was a much harder
task.   Probably the stones were lifted to their position by
underbuilding or wedging.   First one end was raised, then
the other, and thus, slowly but surely, the stones were
brought to a level with the top of the uprights, and were
pushed into position by means of levers.   No doubt thousands of men were employed in the work, and years elapsed
before the temple was complete.

6. If we open some of the more recent tombs, we shall
find remains of a people whom we may call " Bronze "
men, or Celts.   When they sailed across the North Sea to
this island, some seven or eight centuries before the birth of
Christ, they brought with them weapons of bronze—that
is, a mixture of copper and tin.

7. These weapons were far superior to the stone weapons
of the Iberians, and before long the new-comers were masters
of the island, and its old inhabitants were their slaves.

Some of the conquered race took refuge in South Wales and South-west Ireland, where their descendants may be seen to this day. It is said that the name Erin, which is often given to Ireland, comes from the word Iberian.

8. The Celts were a much superior race to the Iberians

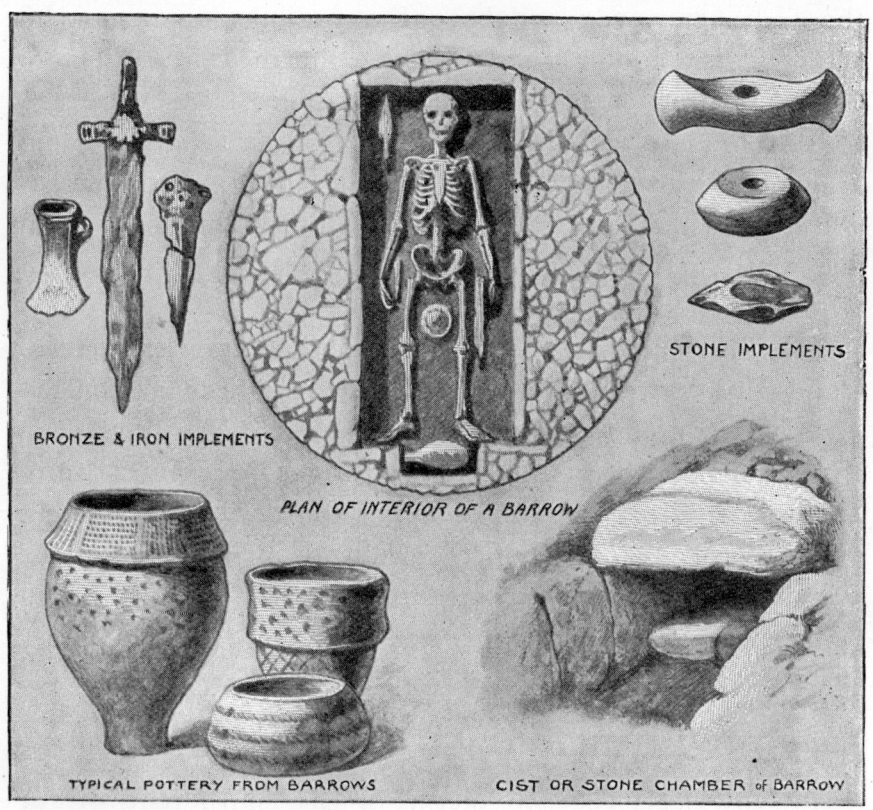

BRONZE & IRON IMPLEMENTS

STONE IMPLEMENTS

PLAN OF INTERIOR OF A BARROW

TYPICAL POTTERY FROM BARROWS

CIST OR STONE CHAMBER of BARROW

in both mind and body. They were tall, blue-eyed, light-haired, fond of fighting, and skilful in battle. They were divided into many tribes, each with its own prince or chief. At the time when the Romans came to this country the Celts of the British Isles consisted of two great nations—

the Cymry in the southern part of Britain, and the Gaels in the Highlands of Scotland and in Ireland.

9. You already know that the scanty knowledge which we possess of the Iberians is obtained from a study of the remains dug out of their burial-places. In the case of the Celts, however, we have the writings of men who actually visited our land. In the fourth century before Christ a learned man named Pytheas sailed from Marseilles to Britain in search of tin. On his return he wrote an account of the island. In it he tells us that Britain was a land of cloud and rain, that the inhabitants grew corn and roots for food, and made an intoxicating drink out of wheat and honey.

10. Two hundred years later another traveller named Posidonius visited Britain. He describes the Britons as civilized, fond of strangers, and skilful in working tin. Less than a hundred years after the visit of Posidonius, Julius Cæsar, the great Roman general, invaded these islands. He wrote an account of the Celts of Britain in a book which is read in most schools where Latin is taught.

———————————◆◆———————————

3. HOW THE ANCIENT BRITONS LIVED.

1. Now let us try to picture a day in the life of the ancient Britons. We shall have to carry our thoughts back more than two thousand years. We must think of a land without many people in it, without stone houses or towns such as we now know, without roads, railways, bridges, mines, factories, or great stretches of tilled land.

2. Let us suppose that we are on board the ship of a hardy trader from the south of Europe, and that we are drawing near to the coast of Britain. We see before us the white cliffs gleaming in the sunlight, and soon our ship runs ashore on a strip of sand. Looking inland, we see a vast green forest, the tall tree-tops waving in the sea breeze.

3. The captain of our ship is an old trader ; the Britons know him and trust him, so he makes his way fearlessly to the nearest " town," and we go with him. We plunge into the dark shades of the forest, and follow a narrow track that winds hither and thither through the dense undergrowth.

4. We are armed, for in the thickets and in the caves of the rocky hillocks lurk the gray wolf, the fierce boar, the black bear, and the wild cat. Now and then a startled deer gazes at us for a moment, and bounds away into safety. We pass by a stream in which herons are fishing and beavers are building. Overhead we see hawks sailing by, and from a neighbouring marsh we hear the boom of a bittern.

5. On we go, and at length we reach a great cleared space. The trees have been felled, and some of the land is under tillage. Horses, sheep, and oxen are quietly grazing, and here and there we see patches of yellow grain. Half a mile away is the " town." All round it is a trench or moat, with an earthen wall on which is a stockade of oak logs. As we draw near to the entrance we see the pointed roofs of many huts, and observe thin lines of blue smoke curling up into the air.

6. We enter the town by a zigzag road, and pass by the beehive-shaped dwellings, which resemble the Zulu kraals of our own day. The walls are made of thin, straight boughs tied together, daubed over with mud and lined with clay; the roofs are thatched with rushes, straw, or bracken. The floors are of earth, or perhaps lined with thin slates. In the middle of each hut is a wood fire, and the smoke escapes by a hole in the roof. Roughly-hewn blocks of wood serve as table and chairs, and round the walls are beds of soft moss, with deer-skins or fleeces as coverings.

7. Before the door of one of the huts a British woman sits grinding corn with a *quern* or hand-mill. She has blue eyes and fair hair, and wears a tunic of dark-blue cloth. Sturdy little boys, scantily dressed in strips of bear-skin, play about the hut, and a girl is coming towards us with a roughly-made water-pot on her head. Peeping into the hut, we see wooden platters and bowls on the block of wood that serves for a table. We see also an old woman busy about her household duties. Notice, she is boiling water. She makes stones red-hot in the fire, and then drops them into an earthen pot filled with water.

8. Now we reach a long, low dwelling with rough oaken walls. Big mastiffs and wolf-hounds, used for hunting, lie before the door. We enter, and notice that the walls are covered with skins. Round shields of hide with shining metal knobs, spears with bronze heads, and bows with quivers of reed arrows tipped with flint are hung up on the walls. This is the home of the chieftain of the tribe.

9. He comes forward to welcome us. He is a tall, well-

made man, with blue eyes, fair hair, and a long moustache. Over his tunic he wears a mantle of cloth, and round his neck is a twisted *torque* or rope of gold. Where his skin is bare, we notice that it is painted with patterns of blue. He greets us in a friendly manner, and an Iberian slave hands us a drinking-cup filled with mead.

10. His wife comes forward too. Over her tunic is a scarf of red-striped plaid fastened by a pin of bronze. A string of dusky pearls adorns her neck, and spiral rings of silver shine on her fingers. The ivory bracelet and the amber beads which she proudly wears have been brought from afar by the traders who visit the " town " from time to time.

11. There is no idle person in the place. The chieftain's wife has work to do as well as her poorer sisters. She has to spin, to knit, to weave, to dye, to sew, to cook, to grind corn, and to milk the cows. Most of the men are away tending the flocks and herds or harvesting the grain. When the grain is reaped, the ears will be stored in underground chambers, and every day a supply will be brought forth to be pulled, roasted, and beaten out with a stick.

12. Here we see a man cleverly weaving baskets of wicker-work; and yonder is a fisherman carrying on his back a coracle, or wicker-work boat covered with skin. You may see the fishermen of certain Welsh rivers using similar boats to-day. This man has been fishing in the neighbouring stream. Over his arm he carries a net, and in his hand is a paddle.

13. Here is the metal-worker's hut. He melts copper and tin over his fire, mixes them together, and then pours

the bronze into moulds. Thus he makes the heads of axes and spears. Another worker hard by is busy chipping flints which have been brought from a quarry in the chalk hills. He fashions them skilfully into arrow and hammer heads. Yonder is a man kneading out yellow clay with which to make pottery.

14. Such was the Briton of Kent more than two thousand years ago. We must not, however, suppose that all the Britons were of this type. Further inland they were simple herdsmen, living on the flesh and milk of their cattle. Still further inland they were little better than savages. They lived by shooting deer or snaring birds, and wrapped their blue-stained limbs in the skins of the wild animals which they hunted.

4. ROMAN REMAINS.

1. There is scarcely a part of England where evidences of the Roman occupation of Britain cannot be seen. Roman walls still stand in many places, and on some of them we may see cut deeply into the stone the Latin inscriptions which tell us when and by whom they were built. Roman roads still remain, and are used to this day. Roman bridges still cross some of our rivers.

2. Old cities like York and Chester abound in the ruins of Roman buildings. Many of our museums contain Roman altars, Roman coins, Roman statues, and Roman pottery. The city of Bath contains a Roman bath which is still in use. At Silchester a complete Roman city has been unearthed. In various parts of the country, as at Ched-

(1,270)

Building the Great Wall.

(From the design for a fresco by William Bell Scott, H.R.S.A.)

This picture illustrates a scene during the building of the Great Wall which formed the northern boundary of Roman Britain in the days of the Emperor Hadrian (see p. 22). It extended from Wallsend on the Tyne right across the Northumbrian moors, thence to Bowness on the Solway Firth, a distance of nearly seventy miles. The wall was at least sixteen feet high and eight feet thick. Every four miles from one another there were forts, and between them watch-houses within call of each other. The wall was built A.D. 121. About ninety years later—namely, in A.D. 210—the wall was repaired and new fortifications were added by Severus.

THE FIRST INVASION OF BRITAIN BY JULIUS CÆSAR.

(*From the cartoon by Edward Armitage, R.A.*)

worth in Gloucestershire, Roman villas have been laid bare, and we may see for ourselves the beautiful mosaic pavements and broken columns of their houses, their weapons, trinkets, pottery, coins, and inscriptions.

3. These things show us that the Romans lived for a long time in our land. We know that they began the work of conquest in real earnest about the year 43 A.D. The Britons fought long and stubbornly, but they could not stand against the well-armed and well-drilled legions of Rome. They sold their lives dearly, but they sold them in vain, and Britain became Roman, just as India is British to-day.

4. The greatest of all the Roman governors of Britain was Julius Agricola, about whom you read in Book III. He came to this island in the year 78 A.D. In his time Britain really became an outlying part of Rome. Agricola taught the Britons to give up their rude way of living, and to imitate the Romans in all things. Cities, temples, and fine houses, all on the Roman model, were built. British chiefs wore the Roman dress, spoke Latin, and amused themselves as the Romans did beside the Tiber.

5. Where the Romans planted themselves firmly, peace reigned. Heavy taxes were exacted from the people, and many of them were made slaves. They were taught the art of building ; they tilled the soil, delved in the mines, and fished the seas. Cattle, hides, wheat, barley, iron, tin, oysters, hunting-dogs, and many other things, were exported to Rome from Britain. Her trade increased, and she grew rich and prosperous.

6. The Britons under Roman rule lost their fiery courage

and love of freedom, and cared only for fine houses, plenty to eat and drink, and amusements of all sorts. On the hilly frontiers, however, the natives were just as fierce and bold as ever. They still lived under their own chiefs, and made raids upon the Romans whenever a chance offered itself. The Britons of Wales and the Britons of Scotland were never really conquered by the legions of Rome. As far as we know, no Roman ever set foot in Ireland at all.

7. Look at a map of England. Find the Solway Firth on the west coast, and the mouth of the Tyne on the east coast. You will notice that this is the narrowest part of South Britain. Now, right across the hills and valleys from the North Sea to the Solway Firth we may trace a broken line of fire-formed cliffs. If we follow this line, we shall see the remains of what was once a huge wall of stone.

8. For more than seventeen hundred years the winds have hurled themselves against this wall, the rain has beaten upon it, the sun has warmed it and the winter has chilled it, yet parts of it stand to-day. Farmers have taken its stones to build their houses and barns, but even now enough of it remains to give us a good idea of what it was like when it was first built.

9. Look at the picture on page 19. It represents an everyday scene when the wall was slowly rising, about the year 120 A.D. The chief figure is that of a Roman officer with a measuring-stick in his hand. Behind him you see a Roman standard. The officer is angry with a lazy labourer who, instead of doing his work, is wasting his time in gambling. The labourer's wife, carrying her baby, has

just climbed the ladder on to the wall. From the look on her face you see that she expects her husband to be punished for his idleness.

10. Behind the Roman officer you see the soldiers building the wall. You notice that they have to work with their bows and shields beside them. Often they must drop their mallets and trowels and snatch up their weapons to ward off the attacks of the wild tribes living near the wall. Down below you see a party of Britons shooting arrows at the builders. They have wounded one of the workmen, and his comrades are now carrying him away. A soldier on the wall has caught an arrow in his shield.

11. Despite all attacks, however, the wall rises, and at last it is finished. What a vast work it is! For seventy-three miles it crosses the country up hill and down dale. It is eighteen feet high and eight feet wide. In front of it is a deep ditch, and behind it is a rampart of three earthen walls and a ditch. Between the rampart and the stone wall is a broad road, along which the soldiers may move rapidly to the defence of any part that may be threatened.

12. Every four miles along the wall there is a fortified camp, with streets crossing at right angles and gates at the ends of them. Every mile there is a small castle, and between the castles are stone sentry-boxes. Ten thousand men guard the wall. Many of them are Germans, Gauls, Spaniards, and Moors.

13. The building of this wall shows you that the Romans had a hard task in holding the land which they had con-

ROMAN REMAINS IN
BRITAIN.

1. Uriconium, Wroxeter.   2. Carpenter's plane found at Silchester.   3. Gateway to Roman camp, Borcovicus, Northumberland.   4. Newport Gate, Lincoln.   5. Pavement of house at Silchester.   6. Heating apparatus in house at Silchester.   7. Roman pottery found at Silchester.

quered. Two hundred and fifty years after they first came to Britain they still had to keep an army of soldiers along this wall. The spirit of the wild tribes living in the rugged country to the north was not broken. In later years, when the Romans left the country, they swept down with fire and sword upon the defenceless Britons.

---

5. A DAY IN ROMAN BRITAIN.

1. Now let us try to picture a day in Roman Britain. We are suddenly planted down in the island, and, looking about us, we see that a great change has taken place in the appearance of the country since the coming of the Romans.

2. In many places the dense woods that formerly covered the land have been cut down. Broad fields have been carved out of the forests, and now we see them waving with barley, rye, and wheat. Gangs of British slaves are at work in the harvest fields. Britain has become one of the granaries of the Roman empire. Cattle and sheep by the hundred feed on the hillsides; and in Rome they speak of this land as *Britannia Felix*—"Britain the Happy."

3. With the cutting down of many forests the weather has improved. No longer is the island wrapped in steaming mists and the sky always clouded. Many of the rivers which formerly lost themselves in reedy marshes have been embanked, and now flow on as broad, fair streams. The morasses are crossed by causeways, and the Britons loudly complain that their bodies and hands are

worn out in draining the fens and clearing the land for their Roman masters.

4. Look at the road beneath your feet. Broad and straight it runs over hill and valley, across stream and moor and bog. So well made are the roads that some of them are still in use to-day. The Roman engineers have dug down to the rocky crust, and upon this have built layer after layer of squared or broken stones. The upper surface of the road is closely paved, especially in the middle, with large blocks of stone. All this work has been done by the British under the guidance of their Roman taskmasters.

5. While we are examining the road, we hear the tramp, tramp of armed men, and a Roman legion swings by. The soldiers seem to be gathered from all the lands where Rome rules. The olive-skinned Italian marches side by side with the yellow-haired German and the dusky Moor. They are armed with large shields, heavy javelins, and short, thick swords. Their officers, in brazen armour and scarlet cloaks, bestride fine horses. In the midst of the soldiers is the glittering eagle, which they would rather die than have taken from them.

6. Let us follow the legion towards the city of Verulam, which we now call St. Albans. On we go along the broad, white road, now crossing a stream by a bridge, now wading knee deep through the ford of a broad river. Here and there amidst the trees we see the white buildings of a villa, where some British chief or Roman officer lives. Notice his beautiful garden, and his orchard of apples, plums, pears, and cherries. In a sunny spot you will find the

grape vine growing.   Anon we pass a cemetery, with its many earthen mounds.   Beneath those mounds are hollow graves, each with its urn of dark clay filled with the ashes of the dead.

7. On and on we march, swinging to the right or the left as some mounted messenger bearing dispatches for his general spurs by.   At length the roofs of Verulam are seen. Round about the city is a great rampart of stone, and here and there we can see a sentinel leaning on his javelin and shading his eyes as he peers across the plain.   We enter by one of the four gates, and find that the two main streets of the town cut each other at right angles.   As we pass along we see many fine buildings, such as the Britons of old never dreamed of.

8. Here we see the carved pillars of a temple to the god of the sea ; there is a stately shrine to the goddess of wisdom ; yonder are the public baths, with their marble halls.   All Romans love the bath.   They have exchanged the balmy climate of the south for the chilly weather of this northern isle, but in the heated chambers of their baths they rejoice again in the warmth of their native land.   Even their houses are cunningly heated with hot air.

9. Yonder is the court-house.   In front of it the senators in flowing robes, and carrying rolls of parchment, pace to and fro.   Here comes the governor with his guard of soldiers.   Preceding him are his attendants or lictors, each carrying on his shoulder an axe bound up in a bundle of rods.   See how the people in the streets make way for him ! Now a gang of slaves is driven by, and here comes a shock-headed British chieftain who has been captured in border

THE ROMANS BUILDING A FORT AT MANCENION · A·D· 80·

(From the fresco by Ford Madox Brown, in the Town Hall of Manchester. By permission of the Town Hall Committee of the Corporation of Manchester.)

Mancenion, or Mancunium, was the Roman name of the station established on the site of a British fortress at what is now Manchester.

warfare. He is on his way to Rome, where he will be tried before the emperor himself.

10. Yonder is the circus, where the townsfolk throng to see plays performed, or, what they love better, to see gladiators fight to the death. Here on the seats, tier above tier, are Britons who ape their masters in dress and speech. They no longer delight in battle and the chase. With their golden locks cut short and their beards trimmed in the Roman fashion, they spend their days in idle amusement, in feasting, and in gambling. They scorn the old British speech, and talk the slang Latin of Rome.

11. Out of the way! Here comes a drove of rough-coated cattle urged forward by the shouts of their fierce, shaggy herdsmen. We step into a dyer's shop until the cattle have passed. The dyer is busy. His cauldron is set on a brick hearth over a charcoal fire, and in it he is dipping a piece of fine linen, which becomes dyed with the famous Tyrian purple worn by the Romans at their feasts. Now we pass again into the streets, and pause to see the children playing knucklebones on the doorsteps.

12. Here is the lordly town house of a Roman officer. Within, the Roman ladies sew and spin, while their husbands are out drilling, or sitting on the judgment seat. On their dressing-tables are mirrors of polished steel and combs of boxwood. They gird up their robes with brooches of gold and silver, and wear bracelets with costly jewels upon their arms. Pins of bone hold together their long tresses, and on their feet are dainty shoes of silk. Supper is at three. Then the gentlemen will join them. They will recline on couches and eat the dainties of the island, which they

will wash down with draughts of wine from Italian vineyards.

13. Such is the life of the town for the Roman officers and the wealthy Britons. The British peasants, however, are slaves. They till the land for their Roman masters ; they build for them roads, palaces, walls and towers of defence. In the marshes of the Medway and on the banks of the Nen they fashion earthenware or glass vessels of yellow, ruby, and blue. They work in the mines of iron, tin, copper, and lead, and smelt the ore in charcoal furnaces. They learn how to paint pictures, carve statues, work bronze, and make pavements of wonderful colour and form.

14. Some of them serve in the army in the distant parts of the empire, or on the wild frontiers of their own land. Most of them, however, are peaceful workers. They have not learned the arts of warfare, but the day will soon dawn when they will have to take up the unfamiliar bow and arrow, sword and shield, to beat back the fierce foe.

15. Rome is even now growing weaker. Fierce tribes from the north are pushing on towards the gates of the great city itself. Soldiers are drafted from all the Roman world to defend the heart of the empire, but in vain ; and at last the Roman emperor sends letters to the cities of Britain, telling them that they must provide for their own safety. The last of the legions leaves British shores in the year 409, amidst the sighs and tears of the inhabitants. All hope goes with them, for the British are as sheep without a shepherd. Thus Britain is left to her fate, and for two hundred years darkness closes around her.

6. HERE ENGLISH HISTORY BEGINS.

1. To-day we will visit one of the most famous places in all the world.   Come with me to the north-eastern corner of the county of Kent.   You are now in the Isle of Thanet. No doubt you think it a poor sort of island, for it is only cut off from the mainland by a little river and a brook that you can easily jump across.

2. When, however, the Romans ruled in Britain, Thanet was a real island.   A broad arm of the sea ran between it and the mainland, and the ships of the time could easily sail through the channel.   On the mainland, at the northern end of the channel, the Romans built the fortress of Re-culvers ; at the south end they built the strong castle of Richborough, the ruins of which are still to be seen.   The north wall is still about twenty-three feet high.   Rich-borough was the usual landing-place of travellers from Gaul.

3. On the island of Thanet, not far from the walls of Richborough, is Ebbsfleet, the spot which I have brought you to see.   Perhaps you will say, "There is nothing to see after all."   Certainly there is not much.   There are merely a few gray cottages dotted over a stretch of higher land, cut off from the sea by a meadow and a sea-wall. Here, however, we stand on sacred ground.   Here English history begins.   This spot was the first in all Britain to feel the tread of English feet.   Why did the English come here ?

4. To answer this question we must go back to the time when the Roman soldiers withdrew and left Britain to its fate.   Sad indeed was the condition of the land.   Fierce

foes, formerly held back by the Romans, now attacked the country on every side. The Picts and Scots swarmed over the great Roman wall, and carried fire and sword through the land even to the gates of London. English pirates swooped across the North Sea, sailed up the estuaries, and landed their crews to burn, kill, and rob without mercy.

RICHBOROUGH CASTLE.
(*From the picture by Clough Bromley.*)

5. The Britons, though for the most part unused to arms, fought bravely, but they could not withstand the robber bands. In their despair they sent a letter to Rome. It was called "The groans of the Britons," and in it they said: "The savages drive us into the sea, and the sea casts us back upon the savages. Our only choice is whether we shall die by the sword or drown, for we have none to

save us." Rome could do nothing to help them; and though brave princes rose up to lead them against the foe, the Britons were disunited, and made but little headway against their enemies. King Arthur, about whom you read in Book II., was perhaps the most famous of these princes.

6. You already know the story of Hengist and Horsa. You know that Vortigern, the King of Kent, was hard pressed by the fierce northern tribes, and that he determined to set a thief to catch a thief. He sent to the English pirates, and begged them to come and help him. Little did he think that by so doing he was paving the way for an English conquest of his country. Hengist and Horsa came at Vortigern's call. Their ships sailed up with a fair wind to the gravel spit of Ebbsfleet, and there they landed and formed a camp. I need not tell the story all over again. You remember that Hengist and Horsa, at the head of their men, drove away the Picts and Scots, and then turned their arms against the Britons. After a long war Hengist became master of Kent, and thus set up the first English kingdom in Britain.

7. What Hengist had done other English war-chiefs thought that they could do too. They swarmed across the North Sea, and in various parts of the country set up little kingdoms of their own. One hundred and fifty years after the landing of Hengist and Horsa the English ruled in this land from the North Sea to the Severn, and from the English Channel to the Firth of Forth.

8. Britain had become England. No longer was it the land of the Britons, but the land of the English. Now, who were these English? Where did they come from,

and what manner of people were they? Look at this map. It shows you the fatherland of the English race. You will see the names of three tribes on the map—the Saxons, the Angles, and the Jutes.

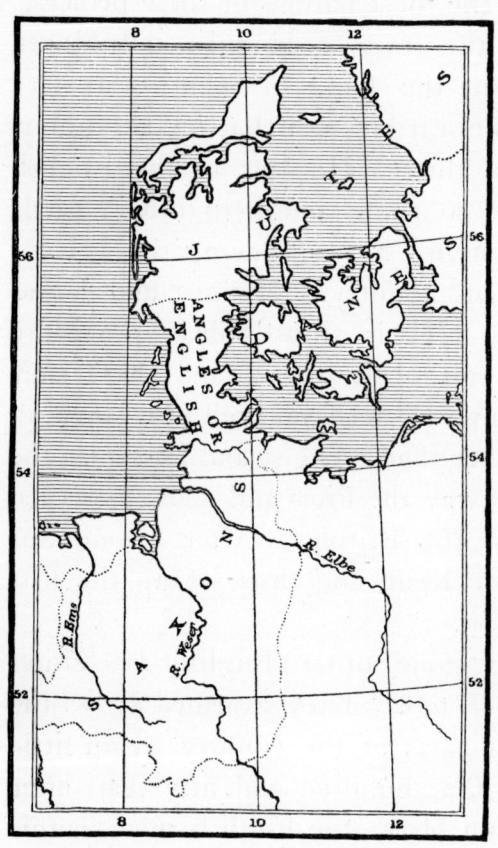

THE FIRST HOME OF THE ENGLISH.

9. The Saxons lived about the lower courses of the German rivers the Ems, Weser, and Elbe. The Jutes lived in the northern half of the peninsula which separates the North Sea from the Baltic Sea. Their first home is still called Jutland—that is, the land of the Jutes. The Angles dwelt between the Saxons and the Jutes, in the heart of the same peninsula.

10. Now all these tribes were akin. They had the same blood in their veins and spoke the same speech. They all had the same kind of religion and government, and they lived in the same kind of country. It was a "wild waste of heather and sand, girt along the coast with sunless woodland, broken here and there by meadows which crept down to the marshes and the sea."

11. Here they lived a hard life as hunters, fishers, and farmers. The barren soil drove them to the sea, and in their long, swift keels they harried the coasts of richer lands, and returned laden with spoil. A Roman poet sang of them : "Foes are they fierce beyond other foes; the sea is their school of war and the storm their friend ; they are sea-wolves that live on the plunder of the world."

12. The Jutes were the smallest of the three tribes, but they were the first to settle in England. Hengist and Horsa and the men who founded the kingdom of Kent were Jutes. The Angles conquered the whole of East Britain from the Stour to the Forth, and gave their name to the whole land. The Saxons spread southward from the Stour to the English Channel, and westward to the Severn and the Mendip Hills. The countryman of Southern England gets his fair hair, his blue eyes, and his bluff, hearty nature from his Saxon sires.

7. THE MAKING OF ENGLAND.—I.

1. To-day we will visit the University Library of Cambridge. Let us make friends with the librarian, and ask him to show us some of the manuscripts of great age and priceless value which are kept in the library. Amongst them are two copies of the oldest book of English history which we possess. This book is written in Latin, and was the work of a Welsh monk named Gildas, who has been called " the wisest of the Britons." He is said to have been born less than seventy years after the first settlement of the Jutes.

2. Gildas wrote his book in a monastery of Brittany, to

PEVENSEY CASTLE.

This castle is of Roman origin, and was built to resist the attacks of the Saxons. It is largely constructed of Roman bricks, and is the castle referred to on page 38 as being captured by the Saxons under Ælle. A thousand years ago, the sea, which is now a mile away, came up to its walls. Close by William the Conqueror landed in 1066.

which he retired about the year 550, when the Britons were hopelessly beaten and the English were firmly established in the land. Gildas gives us an account of the conquest of Britain, and no doubt he derived much of it from the lips of men who had actually taken part in the great struggle. Let us see what we can learn from his pages about the making of England.

3. We learn first of all what I told you in the last lesson— namely, that Britain was conquered by independent bands of Angles, Saxons, and Jutes, who pushed across the North Sea in their war-keels. The Jutes were the first to make a permanent settlement, but they were destined to occupy a much smaller part of Britain than the Angles and Saxons. Their conquests only extended to Kent, the Isle of Wight, and part of what is now Hampshire. Kent took the Jutes twenty-five years or more to subdue. By the end of that time, however, the English kingdom of Kent was firmly founded.

4. The Saxons had been the first English pirates to trouble the shores of Britain. They had made many plundering raids before the departure of the Romans, and were well known to the Britons, who therefore called all the invaders by the common name Saxon. To this day the Celt of Wales and of the Highlands of Scotland speaks of his English neighbours as Saxon.

5. The Saxons made their first invasion of Britain about twenty-seven years after the landing of the Jutes. They were led by their chief Ælle and his son Cissa, and they landed on the shores of what is now Sussex, at the very spot where the Normans disembarked five hundred and seventy-five years later.

6. The coast was guarded by a Roman fortress, but it fell before the fierce and pitiless Saxons, who, Gildas tells us, "left not a Briton alive." Then Ælle founded the kingdom of the South Saxons, which still keeps its name as the county of Sussex. It was always a small kingdom, because it was prevented from expanding northward by the great forest of the Weald.

7. The third invasion was on a much larger scale. It, too, was an invasion of Saxons, and it took place about twenty years after the descent of Ælle and his followers. The leader of this invasion was Cerdic, from whom nearly all the kings of England are descended. Cerdic and his men landed on the shores of Southampton Water, and at once began fighting their way northward. The kingdom which they established was that of the West Saxons, or Wessex, so called because it was formed to the west of Sussex.

8. Under Ceawlin, who became King of Wessex in the latter half of the sixth century, Wessex was greatly extended, and the three Roman cities—Bath, Gloucester, and Cirencester—were captured. The founding of Wessex is most important, for it afterwards became the leading kingdom of England.

9. Gildas writes in a very sad and gloomy strain when he tells us of the triumph of the Saxons, and dwells upon the vices and weaknesses of his own countrymen which prevented them from driving out the foe. He tells us of the awful slaughter, the spoiling and burning of homesteads, the leading into captivity, and all the shame and horror of the conquest.

10. The Saxons, he tells us, showed no mercy even when the battle was won. "Some of the Britons," says Gildas, "were caught in the hills and slaughtered; others were worn out with hunger, and yielded to a life-long slavery. Some passed across the sea, others trusted their lives to the clefts of the mountains, to the forests, and the rocks of the sea."

11. We must not, however, imagine that the Saxons simply came, saw, and conquered. They had to fight very hard indeed to establish themselves in the land, and frequently received severe checks at the hands of the British. The famous hero Arthur, who defeated the Saxons with great slaughter at Mount Badon, is not mentioned by Gildas, who died in the year of this victory.

---

8. THE MAKING OF ENGLAND.—II.

1. Meanwhile the ruthless strangers from across the sea were making settlements in other parts of England. Gildas does not give us clear information about the founding of these kingdoms, so we must piece the story together from the confused accounts of other writers.

2. Between the Thames and the Stour a band of Saxons founded the kingdom of the East Saxons, or Essex. To the north of the Stour the third great division of the invaders established itself. This was the Angle or Engle, who founded three kingdoms, which taken together then formed the greater part of the conquered land. For this reason the whole land was called England, and not Saxony.

3. The great Angle kingdoms were East Anglia, which consisted of the North Folk and South Folk, represented by the modern counties of Norfolk and Suffolk, and Middle England or Mercia. In Book III. you read how Ida, the Angle, seizing Bamburgh Castle, founded the kingdom which was called Northumbria.

4. Now look at this map. It shows you the various English kingdoms as they existed at the end of the sixth century. You notice that the whole western side of the land from the Clyde to the English Channel was in the hands of the British. As you will see from the map, the rest of the country was divided into seven kingdoms.

5. Warfare was no longer waged between Briton and Englishman for possession of the land, but between Englishman and Englishman for supremacy between the various kingdoms which Angle, Saxon, and Jute had founded. The story of our land for the next three hundred years is the story of how these kingdoms became unified—that is, welded into one great kingdom.

6. In the beginning of the ninth century a king of Wessex made himself overlord of the whole land. The work of union was interrupted for a time by the invasions of the Danes ; but these invasions themselves were in the end the greatest help towards unity, for they caused all Englishmen to join together, under the House of Wessex, to subdue the Danes. The first real king of all England was Alfred's descendant, Edgar, and after him, Cnut the Dane made England the centre of an empire which included Denmark and Norway. The English people owe much of their great success to the fact that their land was unified

early in its history, and that when the tribes on the Continent were fighting and struggling for union, England was united and at peace with herself.

7. We cannot follow the story of the ups and downs of the various kingdoms in detail. Sometimes a strong king would make his power felt far and wide ; but his lordship was far from secure, and frequently the conqueror of one day was the hunted fugitive or the mangled corpse of the next. For example, about the year 597, Ethelbert, King of Kent, made himself supreme over Sussex, Kent, Essex, East Anglia, and Mercia. His supremacy, however, was not long-lived.

8. Ethelfrith, the King of Northumbria, soon urged his kingdom to the front. As you already know, he was slain in battle, and then Redwald, King of the East Angles, became prominent. Northumbria, however, became so powerful under Edwin that he was acknowledged as overlord from the Forth to the English Channel, with the single exception of Kent. After the death of Edwin in battle, Mercia, under her heathen king Penda began to assert itself ; but Penda was slain in turn, and once more the star of Northumbria was in the ascendant. It blazed for thirty years, and then paled its fires for ever.

9. At length the rivalry was narrowed down to a struggle between Mercia and Wessex, and during the greater part of the eighth century Mercia was the more powerful. Offa, a Mercian king who reigned from 755 to 794, was the greatest king whom England had yet seen. He pushed back the Britons, and built a dike from Chester to Chepstow to mark the western boundary of

his kingdom. He also drove the men of Wessex south of the Thames, and was acknowledged as the supreme lord of England.

10. The sceptre, however, passed away from Mercia with the death of Offa, and fell into the hands of Wessex, a state that had chiefly busied itself in winning broad lands from the Welsh rather than in striving for supremacy among its kinsmen. In a later lesson we shall learn how the ruler of Wessex became overlord of all England.

---

9. HEATHENS AND CHRISTIANS.

1. You already know that when the English came to Britain they were a rude, uncivilized race of warriors, farmers, and sailors. They could not build fine houses, they could not write or read books, they could not paint pictures or carve statues. They saw with wonder the fine Roman cities, but they did not at first dwell in them, for they hated town life and loved the open country.

2. The newcomers found themselves the possessors of a fertile and civilized land. Their own country was poor and barren. In Britain they found broad meadows and fine hill pastures, with flocks of sheep and herds of cattle. Orchards and vineyards and great cornfields were common; there were ironworks, tin mines, quarries, potteries, glass-works, and fisheries. Splendid stone-made roads good for travelling all the year round crossed the country; the rivers were bridged and the fords were staked or stone-bedded. There were safe and convenient ports, and there was a

large trade with the Continent in grain, metal, jet, slaves, hounds, and horses.

3. To this rich land came the English, a race of uncivilized heathens. Their religion was fierce, warlike, and bloodthirsty. They believed in many gods, such as *Wodin*, the wisest of the gods and the father of victory ; *Thor*, the thunder-god ; *Tiu*, the god of war ; *Freya*, the goddess of love ; and many others. The days of the week—Tuesday, Wednesday, Thursday, and Friday—still retain for us the names of the four chief gods of the English. Tuesday is Tiu's day ; Wednesday, Wodin's day ; Thursday, Thor's day ; and Friday, Freya's day.

4. The English also believed in ogres or giants, in dwarfs who dwelt beneath the ground, making magic weapons and charmed rings, and in elves, the fairies of the woods, meadows, and wells. They carefully buried or burned their dead, lest the angry souls should haunt the spot where their uncared-for bodies lay. By the side of the dead man they placed food and drink, weapons and slaughtered horses, so that he might have the means of hunting and feasting in the future life.

5. The English believed that after death they would live in Valhalla, where they would spend the days in the fierce delights of war, in cleaving helmets and hacking limbs. At nightfall their wounds would be healed, and they would sit feasting on a great boar whose flesh never got less, and drinking mead out of the skulls of their enemies.

6. Cowards, they believed, would be shut out of Valhalla, and sent to dark places of famine and torment. They thought that they could never attain to Valhalla by dying

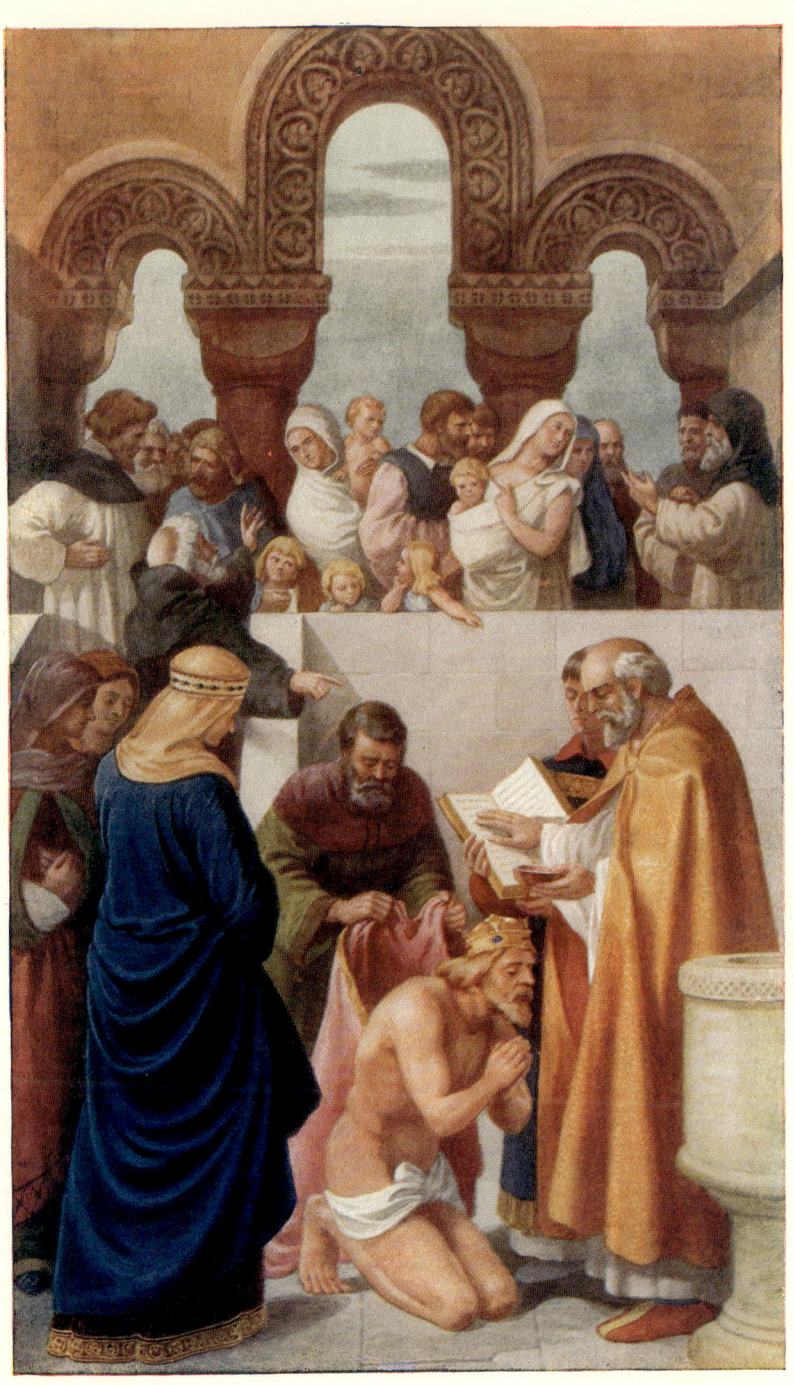

Baptism of Ethelbert.
(*From the fresco in the House of Lords by William Dyce, R.A.*)

peacefully in their beds. When a peaceful death seemed to be their lot, they would wound themselves with knife or spear, or throw themselves from the cliffs, or set sail in a little boat to wrestle with the sea and the storm. They believed that, after perishing amidst the waves, they would pass at once to Wodin's halls.

7. Valhalla, they believed, would at last pass away, and another heaven would take its place. Then this, in turn, would disappear. Monsters would devour the sun and the moon, tear up the mountains and trees, and blot the stars out of heaven, until one wide shoreless sea covered the whole world. Then after a terrible fight, a huge wolf would devour Wodin and the other gods, and finally the wolf's jaws would be torn asunder and everything would utterly perish.

8. In this fierce, hopeless belief the English remained for nearly one hundred and fifty years after they first settled in this country. During this time they were conquering the Britons, and either driving them into the fastnesses of the west or completely wiping them out. We must think of this hundred and fifty years as a time during which all the middle and east of the country entirely passed into English hands. Towards the close of the sixth century, as you already know, the English conquest was complete.

9. Then came the wondrous change wrought by Augustine and his band of monks. I have already told you how they came to visit this land. I am sure you will remember the story of Gregory and the slave boys at Rome. You will remember, too, how Ethelbert became a Christian, and how, one by one, the other kings followed his example.

One hundred years after the coming of Augustine all England had been won from its old heathen darkness.

10. Rome was then the great centre of learning and education. Bands of monks came from Rome to this country and settled down in monasteries. They taught the people, not only the truths of religion, but the arts of reading, writing, building, painting, and healing the sick. Students flocked to these monasteries, eager to learn, and soon the people began to make progress in civilization.

11. In the course of time the English inhabited the old Roman cities once more, and many of them became skilful craftsmen. Churches were built, at first of wood, then of stone. The laws were made more merciful, the people threw off their fierce, lawless ways, tillage was improved, and trade began to be important.

12. In Book III. you were told the story of St. Aidan, in order to show you that there was Christianity in this land before the coming of the Roman monks. The Britons in their highlands of the west were Christians, and so were the people of Ireland, which was then called the " Isle of Saints." Irish monks, you will remember, established their headquarters at Iona, and from their little island home made missionary journeys amongst the people of Scotland and of north England.

13. Long before Augustine came to this country, missionaries were wandering from one cluster of huts to another over the wild moors of Yorkshire preaching the Christian faith. At certain places along the coast monasteries had been set up.

The Last Chapter.

10. THE FIRST GREAT ENGLISH SONG.

1. Let us visit the site of one of the monasteries which was founded before the coming of Augustine. We sail northward along the Yorkshire coast until we come to the mouth of the little river Esk. It enters the sea between two hills which end in steep cliffs. On both banks of the river, and straggling up the heights, is the old town of Whitby.

2. Some of you may have spent a holiday in the town. If so, you will remember the red-tiled cottages of the fishermen, the gray walls of the quays and houses, the little bridge, and the ships sailing up the river at high tide. Perhaps you will also remember the gray ruins that crown the east cliff. There, on a bleak table-land without a single tree, stands all that remains of the ancient abbey of Whitby.

3. Old as these gray walls are, there were once buildings on this spot much older still ; for it was on this wild cliff, in the year 566, that a royal lady named Hilda founded an abbey for monks and nuns. In this abbey the first great English song was composed and sung. Hilda did not compose it, nor did any one of the monks and nuns who lived pious lives within its walls. No ; the great song flowed from the lips of a humble man who tended the cows and slept in the byre. He was the first of the long and glorious roll of English poets. His name was Cædmon.

4. Now, it was the custom in those days to pass the harp round at feasts, and require each of the guests to sing a song to amuse the company. Cædmon was a simple, unlettered man, and when he saw the harp coming towards

WHITBY ABBEY AS IT IS TO-DAY.

him he was so nervous that he used to rise from the table and go quietly to his byre, so as to be out of the way.

5. Once when he had done this, he fell asleep, and dreamed that One came to him and said, " Cædmon, sing Me something." " I know not how to sing," replied the man, " and for this cause left I the feast." " Yet," said the vision, " you must sing to Me." " What shall I sing ? " asked Cædmon. " Sing," the vision said, " about the beginning of created things." At once Cædmon began a hymn in praise of the Creator of the world. Beautiful thoughts flashed into his mind, noble words flew to his lips ; he had composed the first great English song.

CÆDMON'S CROSS AT WHITBY.

Noe friſme. þþa hine nergend heht. hynde þam hal
gan. hæðron cyninge ongan. ofoſt lice þ hof þyrcan.
micle merſe ciſte. magum fægde. þþær þraflic þing.
þldoum to þſund. neðe fiſc· hue nefoheon þær. ge
fæð þ ymb þintra þorn. þæn fæſt mæað. gefron
hiſa mæſt. gſno hliſiſtan. innan fuſan. ſonðan
lime. geſaſinod þið flode. þæn noſſ. þy feſhſtan.
þiſ ſynonig cynn. Symle bið þy hſanona. þehit hſeðl
þæſn. ſþauiðe ſæ. ſſnſamaſ. ſpið on bſhſað·

CÆDMON'S HYMN.
(From a manuscript in the Bodleian Library, Oxford.)

6. In the morning he remembered what he had composed in his dream, and told one of the brothers, who brought him to Hilda, the abbess. In the presence of many learned men she ordered him to recite his verses, that his hearers might judge the quality of them. They all agreed that heavenly grace had been conferred on the humble cowherd. Then they explained to him a passage from the Bible, and asked him to put it into verse. Next morning he appeared and repeated the verses which he had composed during the night.

7. Hilda was delighted. She bade him put off his cowherd's dress and don that of a monk. Then he took his place in the abbey, and was taught the whole course of sacred history. He lived in the abbey till he died, and piece by piece he turned the Bible story into harmonious verse, and sang of the judgment-day and the joys of heaven. In all that he wrote, this gentle, retiring monk did not seek his own glory, but strove to draw men away from evil deeds and lead them to do good.

8. If you go to the Bodleian Library at Oxford you may see the manuscript of Cædmon's poems. On the opposite page there is a reproduction of one of the pages of the manuscript. You cannot understand the writing, because the English of Cædmon's day was very different from that of our own time. Nevertheless I think you will be able to recognize some of the words in the following passage. It is part of a poem written by Cædmon, and inscribed upon a stone cross at Ruthwell :—

Rod   wæs ic aræræd ; ahof ic riicne cuningc
[*A-cross was I reared; lifted-I the-noble   king*]

heafunæs   hlafard ; hælda ic ni darstæ
[*the heaven's   lord ;   bend   I-durst-not*]
bismærædu ungcet men boæt gadre ;
[*mocked us   two   men both together*]
ic wæs midh blodæ bistemid
[*I was with   blood moistened*]

9. A well-known writer has turned several of Cædmon's poems into modern English verse. Read the following description which Cædmon gives of the dove sent forth from the ark. I am sure you will think it very sweet and tender.

> " Far and wide she flew
> Glad in flying free, till she found a place
> Fair, where she might rest.   With her feet she stept
> On a gentle tree.   Gay of mood was she and glad,
> Since she, sorely tired, now could settle down.
> On the branches of the tree, on its bearing mast,
> There she fluttered feathers, went a-flying off again.
> With her booty flew, brought it to the sailor,
> From an olive tree a twig, right into his hands
> Brought the blade of green."

10. We ought to be very proud of the writers who have made our tongue so noble an instrument for the expression of great and beautiful thoughts. In their pages they have given us the greatest heritage that a nation can possess. No other land can boast so many great writers. When we think of them, let us not forget the simple cowherd who, more than a thousand years ago, suddenly burst into the first great English song.

ii. AN OLD ENGLISH VILLAGE.---I.

1. The dearest word in the English language is the word "home." No other language has a word which means exactly the same thing. Wherever we may wander, or whatever fortune may bring us, we cannot think of home without tender thoughts. Home is the family dwelling-place, the roof-tree that sheltered our childhood, the abode where our earliest days were spent with our brothers and sisters beneath the sheltering care of our parents or guardians. The word "home" carries with it the idea of a family bond. Now let us see what it has to teach us about our forefathers in the days of long ago.

2. If you look at a map of England, you will find that many places end in the word *ham*, which is an earlier form of the word home. Ellingham, for example, is made up of three words—*Ella*, the name of a great Saxon chieftain; *ing*, meaning the son or sons of; and *ham*, home. Thus Ellingham is the home of the Ellings, or sons of Ella; and Buckingham is the home of the Buckings, or sons of Buck. The syllable *ing* occurs in more than one-tenth of the names of English villages and hamlets. This shows you that the people in a *ham* were at first kinsmen. All the people in a settlement of this kind were related, or were supposed to be related.

3. Other old English place-names end in *tun*, *worth*, and *stoke*. All these names mean an enclosed place of one sort or another. Thus Billington was the *tun* or township of the Billings; Illingworth, the *worth* or protected place of the Illings; and Basingstoke, the *stoke* or stockaded

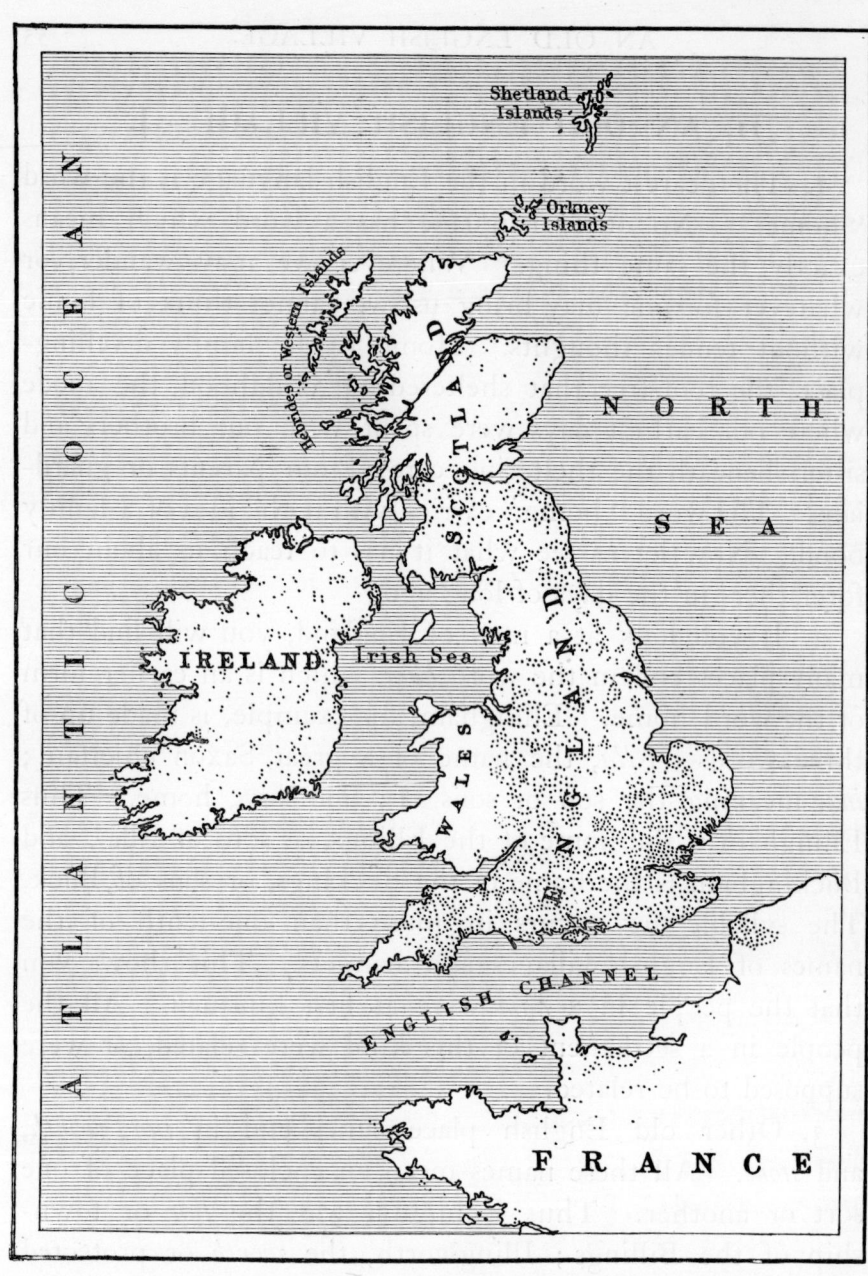

MAP SHOWING POSITION OF PLACES, WITH ENGLISH NAMES.
(*Every dot on this map shows a place with an English name.*)

place of the Basings. Now, these place-names give us a clue to the manner in which the English conquered Britain and settled down in it. They came in tribes—that is, groups of families all united by some loose tie of kindred.

4. When the tribe conquered a portion of the country, the land was divided by lot amongst the conquerors, the leaders, or eorls, taking several shares, and a small knot of brothers or kinsmen taking one share. Then these little groups of kinsmen settled down to the work of their lives as land-holders and land-tillers. They built their rude timber-houses, their byres and barns, and enclosed them within an earthen wall and ditch. The English, in those days, had to live in a protected place, for there were enemies on every side—Britons ready to cut them off if they straggled from their fellows, and wild beasts roaming through the woods in search of prey.

5. You must think of an old English village as belonging to a group of kinsmen all of them freemen, owning the land which they tilled and the plots of ground on which their dwellings stood. Immediately outside the ditch was the village plough-land, which was cut up into strips or balks, divided from each other by unploughed turf. The whole of this plough-land was divided into three great open fields, one of which in turn lay fallow every year ; on another of them wheat, or rye, or oats were grown for food, and on the third barley for drink. Our English forefathers loved to get drunk on strong beer, and this accounts for the large part of the land devoted to the growth of barley.

6. Beyond the plough-land were the meadows on which all the flocks and herds of the village grazed in common,

and beyond the meadows was a wide "mark"—that is, a belt of forest, moorland, or fen. This served as protection to the village, and from it the villagers obtained their timber and fuel. A stranger approaching the village had to blow his horn as he came through the "mark," lest he should be taken for a foe and lawfully slain. Near the town of Reading are three villages which still keep for us the names of these old divisions of the land. Thus *Ear*ley marks the corn-land of the old settlement, *Graze*ley its grazing land, and *Wood*ley its forest.

7. Every village was, as it were, an oasis set down in a desert. There was no trade, and the people of one village had as little as possible to do with the people of another village. The old English loved this state of things. "They live apart," says an old writer, "each by himself." They therefore had to supply all their own wants. They had to build their own houses, spin and weave linen and wool, grind corn, bake bread, brew beer, as well as till the ground and tend the cattle. Further, they had always to be ready to take up sword and shield in defence of their villages, or to follow their chiefs to war.

8. In the middle of each village was a sacred tree or a mound known as the moot-hill, and here the freemen of the place gathered from time to time to manage the affairs of the village. Here they settled how the plough-land and meadow-land were to be allotted, and how the plough-land was to be tilled. If two villagers quarrelled, their dispute was settled by the voice of all the freemen at the moot, according to the "customs" of the place.

9. Each village thus ruled itself. A group of ten villages

formed a *tithing*, and a group of a hundred villages formed a *hundred*. In after times a group of hundreds formed a shire. Every month a *hundred moot* was held, and to this every village of the group sent men to speak for it. Before this court all quarrels between village and village were settled, and all persons charged with crimes were tried.

10. If a man of one village wounded a man of another village, a fine had to be paid, not by the man who did the injury, but by all the men of the village to which the offender belonged. If a man of one village murdered a man of another village, the murderer's village had to pay what was called man-gold to the family of the murdered man. A person in those days was only considered part of his family, and it was the duty of his family to keep him in order, and to bear punishment if he did wrong.

11. Every year there was a meeting of the whole tribe to pass laws, to decide upon peace or war, and to settle disputes which could not be settled in the village moot or the hundred moot. This meeting was called the Witan, or meeting of the wise men, and the head of the tribe was the chief of it.

12. AN OLD ENGLISH VILLAGE.—II.

1. In the home of the English beyond the sea there was no king. Before they sailed, however, each tribe elected a leader, and in England this leader became king of the tribe—that is, " head of the kinsmen." Each king had his bodyguard of warriors, who were called the king's thanes, and to these men the king gave land on condition

that they did him war service. The English villages of Saxmundham and Edmonton, for example, were at first the homesteads of the thanes Saxmund and Edmund, to whom the king gave some of the conquered land. Many of these thanes did not come over with the first war-bands, but left their homes and joined the king after the first settlements had been made.

2. In course of time, and in various ways, the king and the thanes managed to get the ruling power into their own hands. The thanes looked to the king as their lord. To him they owed service, and from him they expected to receive rewards and favours. The thanes became little kings in their own villages, and thus the old free system which the English brought with them from Germany passed away.

3. Now let us look for a moment at the people of an old English village in the tenth century, when this change had taken place. The chief man in the village was the thane or squire. He owned most of the land, and was really the lord of the village. He was of noble birth, and in the old heathen days he was thought to be descended from the gods. Next to him was the priest or parson, who lived on the glebe—that is, on lands given by the thane for the support of religion in the village. The villagers had to pay the priest tithes—that is, a tenth part of their produce—for the same purpose.

4. Next came the yeomen, who were freemen, and what we should now call tenant farmers. They either farmed their own land or farmed their lord's land. In the latter case they had to work for and pay rent to their landlord. Next below them were the cottagers, who were not slaves,

and yet were not free. They worked for their lord, and as wages they had the use of a few acres of ground, which they cultivated in their spare time.

5. Below these again were the labourers, such as herdsmen, barn-keepers, and woodmen. These were serfs, or slaves, and sometimes they were bought and sold just as cattle are to-day. They were either captives taken in war, or poor men who had been obliged to sell themselves into slavery, or those who had been made slaves as a punishment for wrong-doing. Their children were serfs too. In return for their work their lord gave them food and clothes.

6. The village tradesmen, such as the smith, carpenter, leather-worker, and so on, were freemen. Sometimes they took service with the thane of the village, sometimes they carried on business on their own account. Many of the tradesmen, such as the carpenters and potters, travelled from place to place, and had their homes in the towns.

7. From a Dialogue written at the beginning of the eleventh century we get a vivid picture of the daily work of the various labourers in an old English village, and an excellent idea of the state of the country at the time. For example, the *ploughman* says : " I work hard. I go out at daybreak, driving the oxen to the field, and I yoke them to the plough. Be it never so stark winter, I dare not linger at home for awe of my lord ; but having yoked my oxen and fastened share and coulter, every day I must plough a full acre or more. And I do more also. I have to fill the oxen's mangers with hay, and water them, and take out their litter......Mighty hard work it is, for I am not free."

The Ploughman and Ox-herd.

The Shepherd.

The Huntsman.

The Fowler.

COUNTRY SCENES FROM A CALENDAR OF THE ELEVENTH CENTURY.

8. The *shepherd* says : " In the first of the morning I drive my sheep to their pasture, and stand over them, in heat and cold, with my dogs, lest the wolves swallow them up ; and I lead them back to their folds, and milk them, twice a day. I move their folds ; I make butter and cheese, and I am true to my lord."

9. The *ox-herd* says : " When the ploughman unyokes the oxen I lead them to pasture, and all night I stand over them, waking [watching] against thieves ; and then again in the early morning I betake them, well filled and watered, to the ploughman." Neither the shepherd nor the ox-herd nor the other landless men, such as bee-keepers, swine-herds, hinds, goatherds, and barn-keepers, were freemen.

10. The king's *hunter* seems to have been a very contented fellow, for he says : " I braid me nets, and set them in fit places, and set my hounds to follow up the wild game, till they come unsuspecting to the net and are caught therein, and I slay them in the net. With swift hounds I hunt down wild game. I take harts and boars, and bucks and roes, and sometimes hares. I give the king what I take, because I am his hunter. He clothes me well, and feeds me, and sometimes gives me a horse or an arm-ring that I may pursue my craft the more merrily."

11. The *fisher*, who was a freeman, and earned his living by catching and selling both fresh-water and sea fish, says : " I go on board my boat and cast my net into the river, and also cast my angle and bait. I cast the unclean fish away, and take me the clean for meat. The townsfolk buy my fish. I cannot catch as many as I could sell of eels, pike, minnows and eel-pout, trout and lampreys." In the sea

he catches " herring and lax [salmon], porpoises and sturgeon, oysters and crabs, mussels, periwinkles, sea-cockles, plaice and fluke and lobsters." He tells us that it is a perilous thing to catch a whale. " It is pleasanter for me," he says, " to go to the river with my boat than to go with many boats whale-hunting."

12. The *fowler* says : " In many ways I trick the birds —sometimes with nets, with guns, with lime, with whistling, with a hawk, with traps. My hawks feed themselves and me in winter, and in Lent I let them fly off to the woods, and I catch me young birds in harvest and tame them. Many fowlers feed the tamed ones the summer over, that they may have them ready again."

13. The Dialogue also gives us information about various kinds of craftsmen, such as ironsmiths, goldsmiths, silversmiths, coppersmiths, wood-wrights, and shoe-wrights. The latter " make out of hides and fells shoes of various kinds, leather hose and bottles, bridle-thongs and horse-trappings, flasks and hide-vats, spur-leathers, halters, purses and pouches."

14. The *merchant* also gives us a glimpse of his method of doing business. He says : " I go aboard my ship with my goods, and go over sea and sell my things, and buy precious things which are not produced in this country, and bring them hither to you, such as pall [brocade] and silk, precious gems and gold, various raiment and dye stuffs, wine and oil, ivory and mastling [brass], copper and tin, sulphur and glass, and the like. I wish to sell them dearer here than I buy them there, that I may get some profit wherewith I may feed myself and my wife and my sons."

13. ALFRED THE GREAT.—I.

1. Come with me to the grand old university city of Oxford. We are not going to wander through the colleges, or stroll in Christchurch meadows, or go for a row on the Isis. We are going to visit the Ashmolean Museum. In one of the show-cases, carefully preserved, we shall see a priceless jewel. It is a locket made of enamel, enclosed in a setting of gold. On the enamel is the figure of a man, and round the figure are the words, " ÆLFRED ME HAET GEWERCAN," or "*Alfred had me made*." This jewel was dug up some nine hundred years after Alfred had dropped it in the island of Athelney, where, as you already know, he sought refuge from the Danes.

ALFRED'S JEWEL.

2. Now, with this genuine relic of King Alfred before us, let us learn something more about his career than we already know. We will go to the pages of a learned Welshman named Asser, who was greatly beloved by Alfred, and who lived for a certain part of every year in the king's household. Asser wrote a life of his friend the king, in Latin, and translations of this life are to be found in our libraries to-day. Let us turn to a copy and see what it tells us about one who was not only the greatest king of his time, but perhaps the greatest of all our kings.

3. Asser begins by telling us that Alfred was the fourth son of King Ethelwulf, and was born in the year 849 at the royal village of Wantage in Berkshire. He then traces Alfred's descent through noble persons right back to Adam. His mother was Osburh, daughter of Oslac, the famous cup-bearer of King Ethelwulf.

4. When Alfred was three years of age, the Danes first wintered in the island called Sheppey (which means "Sheep Island"), situated in the river Thames between Essex and Kent. In the same year a great army of Danes, with three hundred and fifty ships, entered the mouth of the Thames, sacked London and Canterbury, and put to flight the army of the King of Mercia. Ethelwulf and his son Ethelbald met them in battle at Oakley or "Oak Plain," in the year 851, and after much stubborn fighting won a great victory. Another victory followed soon after, and nine Danish ships were captured, while the others only escaped by flight.

5. In the fifth year of Alfred's life he was sent, with an honourable escort, to visit Pope Leo at Rome. The Pope anointed the child, adopted him as his son, and confirmed him. Two years later Ethelwulf himself journeyed to Rome, taking Alfred with him for the second time, and remaining there a whole year.

6. In the meantime Ethelbald, Ethelwulf's unruly son, formed a conspiracy to oust his father from his kingdom of Wessex. To prevent civil war, Ethelwulf agreed to a division of his kingdom, Kent and Sussex being given to the father, and the remainder to the son. Ethelwulf lived two years after his return from Rome, and on his death Ethelbald became King of Kent and Sussex.

7. In the twelfth year of Alfred's life Ethelbald died, and his brother Ethelbert became king of the reunited kingdom. Ethelbert reigned five years " in peace and love and honour, and went the way of all flesh, to the great grief of his subjects." In 866, Ethelred, the third son of King Ethelwulf, became king, and Alfred, now in his eighteenth year, ruled with him.

8. At this point Asser breaks off his narrative to tell us about Alfred's youth and education. He says: " As Alfred advanced through the years of infancy and youth, he appeared more comely in person than his brothers, as in countenance, speech, and manners he was more pleasing than they. His noble birth and noble nature implanted in him from his cradle a love of wisdom above all things."

9. Then Asser proceeds to tell us the pretty story of how Alfred's mother tried to encourage her sons to educate themselves by the offer of a book of Saxon poetry to the one who was first able to read it. As you already know, Alfred won the prize.

10. In his twentieth year Alfred married a noble Mercian lady named Mucill. Meanwhile, the Danes, growing bolder and bolder, had now become a grievous peril to the land. In the year of Alfred's marriage they marched on York, and, capturing it, pushed into Mercia and wintered at Nottingham. In the twenty-second year of Alfred's life they triumphed over Edmund, King of the East Angles, whom they martyred, and in the next year King Ethelred and Alfred were overcome by them at Reading.

14. ALFRED THE GREAT.—II.

1. Roused by grief and shame at the loss of this battle, the English advanced against the Danes at a place called Ashdown. While Ethelred remained in his tent at prayer, Alfred marched his men on to the battlefield, and, "with the rush of a wild boar," attacked the enemy, who had seized the high ground. The battle was long and fierce, and at nightfall victory rested with the English. Their joy was short-lived : a fortnight later the Danes were again victorious, and soon after another army from over the sea joined them.

2. In the same year Ethelred died of his wounds, and Alfred came to the throne. A month later he fought a fierce battle with a small army and on very unequal terms against his old enemies at Wilton, and was defeated. "Let no one be surprised," says Asser, "that the English had but a small number of men, for they had been all but worn out by eight battles in this self-same year, in the which there died one king, nine chieftains, and innumerable troops of soldiers."

3. Northumbria and Mercia were overrun by the Danes, who now settled in these kingdoms. They parted the land amongst themselves by lot, "sowing and tilling it as their own." Soon they once more attacked their old foes in Wessex. After two years of desperate fighting, Alfred was forced to seek refuge in the woodlands and swamps of Somersetshire. At Athelney, a marsh-girt spot between the Tone and the Parret, Alfred made a stronghold, and from thence "sallied with his vassals of

Somerset to make frequent and unwearied assaults upon the heathen." It was here that Alfred lost the jewel which is now in the museum at Oxford.

4. "The seventh week after Easter," says Asser, "Alfred rode to Egbert's Stone, which is in the eastern part of Selwood Forest. Here he was met by all the neighbouring folk of Somersetshire and Wiltshire, and such of Hampshire as had not sailed beyond sea for fear of the Danes. When they saw the king restored alive, as it were, after such great tribulation, they were filled with joy, and encamped there for one night.

5. "At daybreak of the following morning the king struck his camp and came to Eglea [part of Southleigh Wood], where he encamped for one night. The next morning at dawn he moved his standards to Edington, and there fought by means of a close shield-wall against the whole army of the Danes, whom, at length, with the Divine help, he defeated with great slaughter, and pursued them flying to their stronghold at Chippenham.

6. "Alfred slew all the men, and carried off all the horses and cattle that he could find without the fortress, and thereupon pitched his camp with all his army before the gates of the Danish stronghold. And when he had remained there fourteen days, the Danes, terrified by hunger, cold, fear, and, last of all, by despair, begged for peace. They engaged to give the king as many hostages as he pleased, and to receive none from him in return—in which manner they had never before made peace with any one.

7. "The king took pity on them, and received from them hostages as many as he would. Thereupon the Danes

swore that they would straightway leave the kingdom, and their king, Guthrum, promised to embrace Christianity and receive baptism at King Alfred's hands—all of which articles he and his men fulfilled as they had promised. After three weeks Guthrum, with thirty men chosen from his army, came to Alfred at a place called Aller, near Athelney, and there King Alfred, receiving him as a son by adoption, raised him up from the holy font of baptism. After his baptism he remained twelve days with the king, who, together with all his companions, gave him rich gifts."

8. In the year 879 the Danes left Chippenham, and after a time retired into East Anglia, where they divided up the country. The more warlike and roving spirits amongst them, however, sailed for Gaul and Germany, where they harried less valiant kings ; the remainder settled down quietly in the Danelaw of East England.

9. At this point Asser leaves the history of Alfred's struggles with the Danes to tell us something of the man himself. He tells us that all through his life Alfred was a martyr to ill-health, but that he would not permit the infirmities of his body to prevent him from carrying on his government, from hunting, teaching his goldsmiths and his workmen, his falconers, hawkers, and dog-keepers, building houses after new designs, reciting the Saxon books, and learning by heart, and making others learn, the Saxon poems.

10. Never was king more eager to advance learning and make new discoveries. Our first accounts of Arctic exploration were written by Alfred. He also built new war-galleys, the better to meet the Danes at sea. Alfred's

galleys were swifter, steadier, and higher, and almost twice as long as those of the Danes. Some had sixty oars, some more ; and all were built, not on the Danish model, but according to Alfred's own ideas.

11. Alfred found many of his towns without fortifications and in ruins. He rebuilt London and other towns, as well as two monasteries, one of them at Athelney, where he gathered together monks of all kinds from every quarter, and there settled them. He also built a convent at Shaftesbury.

12. Alfred gave the best of his attention to four things— to law, justice, religion, and education. Asser concludes his book by telling us what Alfred did for justice, which was in a dreadful state at this time. He collected and studied the old laws of the nation. What he thought good he retained ; what he disapproved he left out. Then he laid these before the Witan, and they became the law of the land.

13. Alfred himself translated Bede's " History " into English. He also ordered the old history book now known as the " Old English Chronicle " to be written in English and the story brought down to his own day. This chronicle was carefully kept, chained to a desk in Winchester Minster, and was added to from time to time down to the coronation of Henry the Second. From Bede's book and this chronicle we derive most of the history of these early times.

14. Alfred died in the year 901. Many historians regard him as " the most perfect character in history." He brought his land out of tumult and the darkness of despair into great peace and prosperity. He enlarged the

bounds of Wessex, and saved England from becoming the prey of the Viking. He was a saint and a scholar, a warrior who fought only in defence of his land, and a conqueror who was never cruel. There are few other names in history to compare with his.

------------◆------------

15. THE VIKINGS.—I.

1. In the last lesson you read a great deal about the new invaders whom Asser and the English people generally called the Danes. A better name for them is Vikings, or "creek men." These sea-rovers of Norway, Sweden, and Denmark were so called because they were in the habit of mooring their ships in the bays and creeks, ready to pounce upon peaceful merchant ships passing their shores.

2. The Vikings were of the same race as the English, their language was somewhat similar, and their customs were largely the same. The Vikings of the eighth and ninth centuries resembled in all respects the Englishmen who had conquered Britain in the sixth century. History was repeating itself. Just as the Angles, Saxons, and Jutes had swarmed across the seas, sailed up the rivers, plundered homesteads, fired houses, and slaughtered or carried off into captivity the British inhabitants of the country, so now the Vikings descended upon the English and treated them in the same way.

3. While the English had been converted to Christianity and had become partly civilized, the Vikings still gloried in their descent from Wodin, and revelled in bloodthirsty

Alfred Submitting his Laws to the Witan.
(From the picture by John Bridges.)

warfare. They hated those who had abandoned the old, fierce faith of their fathers for the mild worship of Christ, and fell upon them with especial fury. They shed with joy the blood of priests ; they loved to rob and defile churches. They were a scourge not only to England, Scotland, and Ireland, but to the whole of Europe. France, Italy, Sicily, Russia, and Germany, all were their prey.

4. No race of the ancient or modern world has ever " followed the sea " with such fearlessness and keen delight as the Vikings. The sea was their " swan road," their " Viking path," their " land of the keel," their " glittering home." The ships were their " deer of the surf " and their " horses of the sea." We know exactly what these ships were like, for in the year 1880 a burial-mound was opened at Gökstadt, in Southern Norway, and a Viking ship was unearthed.

5. This ship was sixty-six feet long on the keel, and seventy-eight feet over all. It was fifteen and a half feet in extreme width, three and a half feet deep, was clincher built, and caulked with hair. Its proportions were beautiful, and the whole ship was light, strong, and graceful. When the ship was dug up it was found to contain a chamber in which lay the bones of some forgotten Viking chief, together with the remains of dogs and peacocks. Around the ship's sides were the skeletons of thirteen horses. The prow was turned seaward, as though ready for a voyage.

6. All Viking ships were built on this model, and they varied in length from fifty feet to a hundred and fifty feet or more, and had from twelve to thirty-five seats for the rowers. The larger vessels were decked, and had cabins

THE GÖKSTADT SHIP.
(*From the model in the Pitt Rivers Museum, Oxford.*)

below and a raised platform aft. Usually they were painted white, blue, or red. Over the gunwale were hung the warriors' shields, both to save space and to serve as armour-plate.

7. Both ends of the ship were built alike, so that it could be sailed with equal ease in either direction. Each ship had one mast, with a square sail of woollen stuff, either white or coloured in stripes of blue, red, and green. The high prows of the ship were carved into the likeness of a dragon, a bird, or some other animal. In these somewhat small and not very seaworthy ships the Vikings made voyages which are simply astounding to us to-day. For example, they not only crossed the North Sea to the Orkneys, and to the Humber, but actually discovered Iceland, Greenland, and, according to some writers, North America.

8. Their barks were to be found on all the seas of Western Europe, not only because the Vikings loved the life of a rover, but because they were now obliged to seek new homes in foreign lands. The King of Norway, Harold Fairhair, had overcome the petty kings of Norway one after another, and had made himself supreme king. Many of the petty kings took to their ships, and with their wives and families set off across the " swan road," to find new homes for themselves in distant and better-favoured lands. They were joined by numbers of the freemen, who found their rights taken from them by the king, and heavy taxes placed on their shoulders.

9. We may divide the Viking invasions of England into three periods. The first period was the raiding period. The Vikings sailed up the river mouths, threw up stockaded earthworks as their headquarters, and then scoured the country far and wide, slaying the people, burning the towns and minsters, carving blood-eagles on the backs of the priests, and carrying off cattle and goods till the land was bare and their ships were full of booty. This period lasted from A.D. 787 to about 866.

10. The second period was that of settlement. By the end of the ninth century Vikings had set up kingdoms in Ireland, the Isle of Man, the Orkneys, in Yorkshire and in East Anglia. The largest of these kingdoms was that known as the Danelaw, which, as you know, is the part of England where the Danes were masters. Its greatest extent is shown by the map on page 78. It included the famous five boroughs of Leicester, Lincoln, Nottingham, Stamford, and Derby.

16. THE VIKINGS.—II.

1. You will remember that before the coming of the Danes, England bid fair to become one kingdom under one king. The Danish invasions interrupted this good work; but after the death of Alfred it was resumed, and Edward, his son, was the first king who could claim to be overlord of all Britain. Athelstan, his son, fought a great battle against the Vikings and the Scots, and won a splendid victory at Brunanburgh, after which he had but little trouble from either Scot or Northman. In the reign of Edward and his sons, Athelstan and Edmund, the whole Danelaw south of the Humber was recovered from the Danes.

2. Edgar the Peace-winner, who began to reign nine years after the death of Edmund, was the first real " King of all England." In the year 973, so runs the legend, he was rowed on the river Dee at Chester by eight under-kings, including the King of Scots, who all swore to be faithful to him. "Those who come after me," said Edgar, "may indeed call themselves kings, since I have had such honour."

3. Edgar was only thirty-two when he died, and his children were mere boys. Bitter strife arose amongst the nobles, and in 978 a foolish, cruel, and unjust king, Ethelred the Redeless, or Ill-Counselled, was set upon the throne. Then came a time of grave danger.

4. After an interval of thirty years, the raids of the Vikings began again, and this time on a far larger scale than ever before. The Viking leaders of earlier times had been adventurers of noble blood; now a national host, led by the king himself, was about to conquer the rich and

tempting land beyond the North Sea. The third period, that of conquest, had begun, and England was soon to be ruled by Danish kings.

5. In 991 came the first great blow. A numerous body of Vikings landed, and at Maldon they utterly defeated the men of East Anglia, despite the splendid valour of their thanes, who vowed not to yield, and fell one by one beside the dead body of their leader. In the next year Ethelred was forced to buy a truce, and to permit the Vikings to settle in the land.

MAP SHOWING DANELAW (DANELAGH).

6. In the year 994 a vast body of pirates, under Sweyn Forkbeard, Prince of Denmark, and King Olaf Trygvasson of Norway, sailed in five hundred ships, and strove to take London. They too were bought off, only to repeat their raids again and again, whenever their purses were empty. Actually a tax known as the Danegeld was levied on all the land in England, and the proceeds were handed over to the greedy pirates.

7. The life-blood of the country was rapidly draining away, and in the year 1002 Ethelred ordered the massacre of St. Brice's Day of which you have already read. Amongst the thousands of slain was Gunhilda, the sister

of Sweyn, along with her husband and child. When
Sweyn heard the news, he determined to wrest England
from the cowardly murderer who sat upon its throne.

8. In 1003 his great fleet touched our shores, and for
four years he marched through the length and breadth of
Southern and Eastern England, " lighting his war-beacons
as he went in blazing homestead and town." He was
bribed to withdraw, but soon he returned for a still more
terrible onset.

9. Slowly but surely the Danes gained ground, and
after ten years of fighting, Ethelred was forced to flee to
Normandy, and the Witan chose Sweyn as king in his
stead. Canute, or Cnut, Sweyn's son, succeeded his father,
and carried on the war. After the death of Ethelred, his
son, Edmund Ironside, became the leader of the English.
He was a true hero, and had he come sooner to the throne
he might have saved England from the Danes. Unhappily
he died in 1016, and Cnut became sole King of all England.

10. England has had few better rulers than Cnut, who
was also King of Norway and Denmark. He sent back the
greater part of his invading army ; and the better to govern
his new kingdom, he appointed great earls to rule Mercia,
Northumbria, East Anglia, and Wessex. He restored many
of the best laws of the old kings, and placed Englishmen
in all the important offices. He rebuilt monasteries and
cathedrals, and made a pilgrimage to Rome.

11. Cnut was the first of our kings to maintain a standing
army. From the earliest times the old English kings had
kept at their courts a comparatively small number of *hus-
carles* as a bodyguard. Canute increased their number up

to several thousands ; they constantly attended him, and formed the basis of any greater force that might be needed. All were picked men of valour, on whose fidelity he could absolutely rely. This force never met its match until it perished at Hastings.

12. Cnut died in 1035, and discord broke out at once. His two sons were rough, godless young men, who hated each other bitterly. For a time they divided the kingdom between them, but in seven years both of them were dead. With them the Viking age in Britain came to an end. The Danes who had settled in the country soon became Englishmen, and brought a new strain of courage, daring, and adventure into the English character. In parts of Yorkshire and East Anglia the people, even to-day, remind us, in build and speech, of their old ancestors the Danes.

17. A VISIT TO NORMANDY.

1. To-day we will pay a visit to Normandy, the homeland of the Normans, the fourth and last conquerors of England. We leave Victoria Station, London, at ten in the morning, and at half-past eleven find ourselves on the quay at Newhaven. A fast turbine steamer awaits our arrival, and as soon as the passengers and luggage are transferred from train to boat, we steam out upon the waters of the English Channel. A voyage of sixty-four miles brings us to the harbour of Dieppe, and before four in the afternoon we are stepping ashore. We are now in Normandy, the land of the Normans.

2. Dieppe is a fashionable watering-place built in a valley between two ranges of white chalk hills. It has splendid sands, and during the summer it is crowded with holiday-makers. As we are not now on pleasure bent, we do not linger in Dieppe, but proceed at once to the railway station and take our tickets for Rouen, the old capital of Normandy. Rouen stands on the Seine, forty-five miles from its mouth, and is a busy cotton manufacturing town and seaport. Nevertheless, it is of the greatest historic interest, and contains some beautiful and ancient buildings. Later on, we shall hope to peep into one of them.

3. If we take train from Rouen and travel about Normandy, we shall pass place after place which is famous in our history. The very names of the hamlets on the road-side call up memories of proud nobles or of old battles and sieges. The green fields with their thick hedgerows of hawthorn and bramble, the elms and the smiling apple-orchards, all seem familiar, and are, indeed, the very picture of an English countryside.

4. Amidst the red-tiled roofs of the quaint little market towns rise the stately towers of noble cathedrals; and these, too, remind us of home, for they are the models on which some of our great churches have been built. The square gray towers which we see high up on windy heights over-looking orchard and meadow land are exactly like the keeps of many of our old castles. We need not be surprised at this, for Normandy gave us kings and nobles, and for well-nigh two hundred years was a possession of the English crown.

5. There are two places which I am anxious that you

should see in Normandy. The first of them is the grand old cathedral of Notre Dame at Rouen. It is one of the finest Gothic churches in all the world. We will not stop to admire the wonderful carving over the great central portal, the splendid design of the interior, or the lovely rose windows in the transepts and nave. We will pass at once to the last chapel on the south side of the nave, and stay our steps before the tomb of a great Viking named Rollo or Rolf. Who was this Rolf, and how came he here ?

6. Just about the time that Alfred's sons were winning back the Danelaw in England, a Viking fleet sailed up the Seine under the command of an outlawed chief named Rolf. For forty years this Rolf had been a raider ; now he was to be a conqueror. The man himself was of huge stature, so long of leg and so heavy of body that no horse could carry him ; hence his nickname, Rolf " the Ganger " or walker.

7. Rolf and his men gained possession of Rouen by means of a trick which reminds us very much of the method by which the Greeks captured Troy. Then the Viking began devastating and conquering the country round about, and finally laid siege to Paris itself. Charles the Simple, the King of France, was forced to treat Rolf just as Alfred had treated Guthrum. Rolf was offered Rouen and the district surrounding it, on condition that he would become a Christian and do homage to Charles.

8. When Rolf learned that doing homage to Charles meant that he must kiss the king's foot, he refused to degrade himself by such an act, and once more laid siege

Serf Emancipation.

(From the picture by E. Armitage, R.A. By permission of the Corporation of Liverpool.)

ROUEN CATHEDRAL.

to Paris. At last the French king agreed that one of Rolf's men should do homage in his stead. A Viking was chosen "from the ranks," and at the appointed time this worthy strode up to the stool on which Charles was sitting, but instead of stooping to kiss the king's foot, seized the king's leg and jerked it up to his mouth. In doing so, he tilted the monarch off his seat! Swords were drawn and bloodshed was threatened, but the king poured oil on the troubled waters by declaring that he had received a well-merited lesson.

9. Thus the Vikings got a footing in North France. As they came from the north, it was quite natural that the French people should call them Northmen and their land Northman's land. In the course of time this name was softened into Normandy. The new-comers did not at once unite with the native population, as the Danes had done in England, but held themselves proudly aloof, retaining their own language, manners, and customs. In the end, however, they blended with the people of the land in which they had settled. The heathen pirates became French Christians; the rough Vikings threw off their semi-barbarous ways, and became the most civilized race in Europe, though always turbulent, quick to anger, and eager for battle.

10. Rollo died in 911, and a hundred and fifty years later the Normans had become the foremost race in Europe. They learned or discovered new modes of fighting, and they used new weapons such as the shield, the lance, and the long-bow. They were masterly horsemen, and their fame as warriors spread far and wide. They built magnificent cathedrals, and founded churches and monasteries. The sons

Portion of the Bayeux Tapestry.
(*Showing scenes from the Battle of Hastings.*)

and grandsons of the rough pirate chiefs became courtly knights and learned bishops.

11. In the year 1035, William, then eight years of age, succeeded his father Robert as Duke of Normandy. The early part of his reign was full of perils and alarms, and only after much hard fighting did he force his nobles to acknowledge him as duke. At length, however, he restored law and order throughout the duchy, and then was ready to do those deeds which marked him out as " the most masterly spirit of the most masterly race of his time."

12. Now come with me to the little Norman town of Bayeux, and I will show you something worth travelling many miles to see. You will find Bayeux on the map to the north-west of Caen, the old town in which William was buried. Bayeux is a small place now, but in the time of the Conqueror it was very important indeed. Many of the houses are of wood, and in the midst of them rises a cathedral, said to be the oldest in Normandy. It was originally built by Bishop Odo of Bayeux, half-brother of William.

13. We make our way to the Public Library, which contains a small museum. Here we shall find the precious thing which I have brought you so far to see. It is a huge piece of tapestry, consisting of a strip of linen cloth 230 feet long and 19 inches wide, extended along the side of a large room, and exposed to view under glass. The tapestry, or rather embroidery, consists of a large number of pictures worked with a needle in coloured worsteds. The various scenes illustrate the events which led up to the Norman conquest of England.

14. There are seventy-two of these scenes, showing six hundred and twenty-three persons, seven hundred and sixty-two horses, dogs, and other animals, thirty-seven buildings, forty-one ships or boats, and forty-nine trees. The figures are worked in worsteds of eight different colours, and are still bright and clear. The English are all represented with moustaches, while the Normans have none.

15. This wonderful piece of tapestry is said to be the work of Queen Matilda, wife of William the Conqueror, and her ladies. It is said that the queen's death alone prevented her from adding a scene representing William's coronation. Though we cannot be sure that the work was done by Matilda, we are almost certain that the tapestry was embroidered in the eleventh century, and that it is a faithful record from the Norman point of view of the opening scenes in the conquest of England.

16. I cannot in this book reproduce all the scenes depicted in the Bayeux tapestry, but on page 86 there are some pictures which are typical of the rest. Examine them carefully, and you will see that they illustrate much of what you read in Book III. about the battle of Hastings or Senlac.

17. The pictures of the battle are most interesting. You see William addressing his army, and urging it on to the fight. You also see Odo encouraging the Normans, and William raising his visor to show his men that he is not dead as reported. Then you see the Normans turning on the English, who have broken their ranks to pursue the flying horsemen, and cutting them to pieces. The last two pictures of the series show you the death of Harold and the flight of the English.

18. DOOMSDAY BOOK.

1. The victory at Senlac was only the beginning of the conquest of England. William was crowned king on Christmas morning, 1066, but there was many a hard day's fighting to be done before he could call himself master of England. You read in Book III. how Hereward and other brave Englishmen held out against the Norman in the marshes of Ely. Not until Hereward was overcome did the land have peace.

2. William was a conqueror. He had won the land with his sword, and it was his to deal with just as he pleased. He seized the lands of all the Englishmen who had fought at Hastings, or who refused to acknowledge him as rightful king, and with these lands he rewarded his clamorous followers.

3. He did not, however, give them lands for nothing. "If I give you these estates," said he, "you must promise to serve me. You must promise to provide me with so many fully-armed soldiers, and to send them to fight for me, if I need them, for forty days in each year. You must also pay money at certain times—as, for example, when my son is made a knight, or my daughter is married, or I am captured in war and must be ransomed. When your son comes into possession of your lands, he will pay me money; and if you die without heirs, your land will become mine once more."

4. There was nothing new in this plan, as you already know. Something like it existed in England before the coming of the Normans. All the English thanes had to

do the threefold service of fighting for their king, manning his fortresses, and maintaining his fortifications and bridges.

5. The system which William established in England was fully developed in Normandy, and all the Normans were familiar with it. They therefore agreed to their king's terms, and each knight in turn did homage. He knelt before the king, placed his hands in the king's hands, and made this promise of obedience : " Here, my lord, I become liege man of yours for life and limb and earthly regard, and I will keep faith and loyalty to you for life and death, God help me." The king then kissed the knight, and thenceforth the land or "fee" belonged to him and his heirs for all time.

6. William also granted much land to bishops and other great churchmen in the same way, under the same conditions. Thus from the land which he gave away he provided himself with money and an army. A great deal of the land he kept in his own hands.

7. The knights to whom he had given land now granted "fees" or "fiefs" to their followers and friends, and these vassals, as they were called, made the same promise to their lords that their lords had made to the king. In Normandy and other European countries the vassals had to follow their lords even against the king. Now, William had had personal experience of the terrible mischief which this caused, and was determined to prevent it in England.

8. He therefore ordered all the landholders of the realm, great or small, to meet him on Salisbury Plain, and there swear homage to him directly. Thus he made every one who held land, whether granted by the king or by a lord,

PORTION OF DOOMSDAY BOOK.

own himself the "man" of the king. The vassal was obliged to follow the king, and not his lord, if his lord should quarrel with the king.

9. Here is a photograph of an old piece of writing. It is part of a book that was written some time between the years 1085 and 1087, and is known as the Doomsday Book. If you go to the British Museum, you will be able to see it for yourself. It is preserved very carefully, because it is the most valuable record which we have of our land in Norman times. Now this book was compiled by order of King William, who wished to know exactly how many landholders there were in his kingdom, and what extent of land they owned. The object of this survey was that William might ascertain what amount of taxation his new kingdom could pay.

10. The king's officers went into every hundred, and the inquiry was made so strictly that an old writer tells us "there was not one single yard of land, nor even one ox,

one cow, nor one swine," that was left out. Because the
inquiry was like the day of doom, and every one was ques-
tioned at it, the English called it Doomsday Book.

11. We find from Doomsday Book that the people were
divided into classes. First, there were the barons or king's
vassals—that is, those to whom the king had directly given
land. Then came the barons' vassals—that is, those to
whom the barons had given estates. All these men under-
took to do war service to the king, according to the amount
of their land. The king's vassals, as you know, had also to
pay him certain sums of money at certain times. In the
same way the vassals of the barons had to do service and
pay money to their lords.

12. Next below these nobles and their vassals came the
freemen or tenant farmers, who rented farms from their
lords, and in return gave them money or labour or part of
their produce. Then came the mass of the people, some
of whom had rights, but most of whom were slaves.
Those who had rights were either villeins or cottagers.
The villeins held farms like the freemen, but they were
" tied to the land "—that is, they were not allowed to
give up their farms and go elsewhere, but must always
till the land of their lord.

13. Below the villeins came the cottagers, who had no
land except the gardens round their houses. For these
they had to pay their lord from twenty to thirty shillings
a year in our money, and had also to work on his land at
harvest and other times. Then came the slaves, who belonged to their lords, and were bought and sold just like cattle.
All they received for their labour was food and clothing.

14. Thus, you see, the people of the country might be represented by a heap of stones piled up in the shape of a sugar-loaf. At the top of all was the king, lord of the land and of every one in it. Next below him were the great lords to whom the king had given large estates. Below these, again, were the lesser lords to whom the great lords had given lands. Below them were the bulk of the English people, who had now changed masters. Instead of the twenty thousand English thanes who held the greater part of the land before the Conquest there were now twenty thousand Normans.

19. THE BUILDING OF THE CASTLES.

1. If ever you go to London, do not fail to visit the Tower. If you live in London, you will be sure to know it well. It stands on the north bank of the Thames, about half a mile to the east of London Bridge. Wherever you go within its gray walls, you will see something to remind you of the great doings and the famous people of bygone days. You will see the warders in their quaint old dresses, the crowns and jewels worn by our kings and queens, old swords, armour, and guns, the block on which so many historical personages have been beheaded, and the room in which the poor little princes were murdered.

2. We have not come to see these interesting things to-day. We have come to look at the oldest part of the building. It is called the White Tower, and it was built by William the Conqueror soon after the battle of

THE WHITE TOWER.

Hastings. For eight hundred years and more it has kept watch and ward over the city of London. Of course, it has been much repaired from time to time, but it has not been altered to any very great extent.

3. Now what do we see? We see a great tower or "keep"—"four-square to every wind that blows"—one hundred feet long and one hundred feet broad. It is built of rubble, held together by much mortar, and the

walls are fifteen feet thick. The windows are small and high up ; the door is on the first story, and is reached by a stone staircase. In the days before gunpowder was invented, soldiers within such a keep as this could hold out against a foe just as long as they had food and water. The building could not be battered down, and at best it could only be injured by undermining.

4. The White Tower was the whole Tower of London at first. As time went on, it was made stronger and stronger by adding smaller towers to it, by building strong walls round it, and by digging a ditch or moat outside the walls. In Queen Elizabeth's time it covered a large space of ground, more than twelve acres in all. It is now enclosed by an outer wall with strong towers at the corners, and just outside the wall is a broad ditch or moat. Inside, there are many buildings. The White Tower is the heart of the whole fortress ; if the defenders were driven in from the walls and the towers, the keep would be their last place of refuge.

5. The White Tower is square, but the square keep was not the most common type of Norman castle. In the early twelfth century the round keep was the more usual form. This type of castle grew out of the old English fortification called a *burh*, which consisted of a mound protected by a stockade, and enclosed within outworks of earth and palisading, the whole being surrounded by a ditch. The Normans built a keep or ring of high walls on the mound, and instead of earthworks erected outer walls of masonry. The keep could only hold a small garrison, but in the space enclosed by the outer walls the whole

A Tournament on London Bridge.

(*From an old painting in the Guildhall Art Gallery.*)

of the cattle and stores of a country-side could be collected in case of attack. Gradually the outer fortifications were strengthened, and formed the main line of resistance. Projecting towers were also added, so that the defenders could direct a flanking fire upon the attackers as they approached the walls.

6. Now let us fancy that we are living about eight hundred years ago, and that we are about to pay a visit to a Norman castle. We notice that it is built on a high rock, so as to make it difficult of attack, and to prevent the undermining of its walls. As we draw near to it, we see the great, heavy " curtain wall " frowning down upon us. We cross the moat by a bridge, which is drawn up by chains at night, and whenever danger is nigh.

7. We enter by a great stone portal defended by strong towers. When the castle is shut up, a portcullis or grating of timber and iron is let down in front of the heavy iron-bound door. Above the archway are holes through which shots may be fired and molten lead and boiling pitch poured down on the heads of foes who try to get in. The "curtain wall" itself has a kind of projecting stone gallery running round it, with holes pierced in the footway for the same purpose.

8. Now we enter the outer ward or courtyard. On one side are the stables ; in the centre is the mound where the lord holds his court, and where the guilty are put to death. Another strong gateway with towers protects the entrance to the inner " ward," in which is the great keep, with its walls thirty feet thick at the base and ten feet at the top.

9. There are several rooms in the keep, one above the

THE CATAPULT.

(From the picture by E. J. Poynter, R.A. By permission of Sir Christopher Furness, M.P.)

This picture shows the catapult used in Roman times. There was not much difference between the catapult represented here

other. Stores are kept on the ground floor ; and here, too, is a deep well to supply the castle with water. A spiral staircase, lighted by loophole windows, brings us up to the first floor, where there are quarters for soldiers. Above this is the hall, in which the lord and lady of the castle take their meals and receive their guests. Their sleeping-rooms and the ladies' bowers are in the thickness of the walls. In the uppermost story of all is the kitchen.

10. Many of the Norman castles that survive in England were built during the days of Henry the First. Scores of others were erected in the time of King Stephen, the grandson of the Conqueror. Stephen, as you know, was a weak man, and during most of his reign he was fighting with his cousin Matilda. The barons, held down by the strong hand of William and his sons, openly defied Stephen. They built unlicensed castles, in which they lived as robber chieftains.

11. The Norman kings had often to besiege many of these castles ; but so massive were they that, as a rule, the only way of capturing them was to starve out the garrison. Rufus, Henry the First, and Stephen conducted many sieges, and their method of attack was usually to block up the exits of the castle, and sit down outside until the besieged were ready to surrender. When, however, for some reason or another, the attack was to be pressed home, machines like giant catapults were used to hurl heavy stones into the castles.

12. Some of these machines were worked by twisted ropes, others were like enormous cross-bows, and others again consisted of a balance with a long beam. One end was loaded with heavy weights, and the other end was

dragged down by sheer force.   When this end was released it struck the missile and drove it towards its mark.

13. Sometimes tunnels were dug underground to the foot of the wall, stones were removed from it, and beams of wood with straw and brushwood were substituted for them. When the wood and straw were set on fire the wall fell, and through the breach the attackers entered the castle.

14. Sometimes a wooden tower several stories high was built, and covered with raw hides so that it would not burn. Then the moat, if there was one, was filled up with fagots, and the tower was moved by means of rollers to the foot of the wall.   A drawbridge was dropped on to the top of the wall, and the soldiers in the tower rushed across the bridge and overpowered their opponents.   The Crusaders gained an entry into the town of Acre by using a machine of this kind. Such were the methods by which castles were besieged for nearly three hundred years after the Norman Conquest.

---

20. THE TOURNAMENT.

1. You already know that when the Normans came to England they were the foremost race in Europe.   Compared with the English, they were fine gentlemen indeed. While the English loved to eat and drink more than was good for them, the Normans despised piles of coarse food and hogsheads of strong drink.   Their leaders were far more civilized than the leaders of the English, and loved choice and beautiful things, such as stately houses, noble churches, rich armour, and gallant horses.

2. The Normans were intensely proud, and they looked with contempt on the conquered English. Norman master and English slave were as far apart as they well could be. The Norman in his castle lived and spoke just as he had done in Normandy. He hunted and hawked, played his knightly games, sat on the judgment seat, and feasted in his hall, while the Englishman tended the cattle and toiled in the fields to keep him in plenty.

3. We can learn all this from many of the words which we use every day. Notice these pairs of words : *cow, beef ; calf, veal ; sheep, mutton ; swine, pork ; deer, venison.* The first word of each pair is English, the second is French. Now the English names are those given to the animals when alive ; the French words are those given to them when dead and ready for cooking. This shows us that the English tended and fed the animals when alive, and that when they were dead the Norman cook made them ready for his master's table.

4. Here are some other French words which we often use — *armour, banner, battle, herald, march, lance.* You notice that they have to do with war. The following words are connected with law—*judge, prisoner, summons.* These refer to Church affairs—*Bible, sermon, friar,* and *sacrifice ;* while *baron, duke,* and *prince* are the titles of nobles. Now you see that our very language shows us that the Normans were masters of the land. They were the landowners, the leaders of the army, the judges, the chief churchmen, and the nobles.

5. In the last lesson I told you something about the castles in which the Normans lived. Now let me tell you

about the great warlike sport in which they delighted. It was called the *tournament*, and was held at times of great rejoicing. The tournament which I am going to tell you about is described very fully by Sir Walter Scott in a book called " Ivanhoe," which I hope you will procure and read for yourself.

6. The tournament ground was very much like the football field of one of our great clubs. There was a large oblong space fenced off in the middle, and there were stands along the sides. These stands were beautifully furnished with carpets and cushions for the ladies and nobles who looked on. The people stood on great mounds of turf. They were just as excited as the spectators at a football match are to-day. At each end of the ground, or the " lists " as they were called, there were great gates through which the knights could enter on horseback. Behind one of the entrances were several tents, each with a waving flag and a shield hanging up outside it. These were the tents of the knights who were ready to challenge all other knights to combat.

7. The stands were filled with barons, knights, and squires, and with beautiful ladies in the gayest and richest dresses. The prince, in crimson and gold, mounted on a prancing horse, entered the lists, and then, taking his place on the stand, gave a signal to the heralds, who sounded their trumpets and proclaimed the rules of the tournament. This done, the umpires took their places, and five knights, clad from head to foot in steel and mounted on great war horses, spurred into the lists.

8. The knights first rode up to the tents of the challen-

gers, and each of them touched with the butt of his lance the shield of the knight whom he wished to encounter. Then the challengers rode into the lists, and all was ready. The trumpets sounded, the war horses broke into a gallop, and the knights dashed at one another. Each strove to unhorse the other by striking his helmet or shield fairly in the middle with the lance. Three of the challengers unhorsed the knights opposed to them; the other two couples splintered their lances, but managed to keep their seats.

9. Trumpets sounded again. The beaten knights rode off, and their horses and arms became the property of the victors. A second and third party of knights then took the field, and the warlike game went on; but still the three challengers were not overthrown. The tournament was now likely to come to an end, for no other warrior seemed willing to try his fortune. After a pause, the sound of a distant trumpet was heard, and a new knight appeared. He was Ivanhoe, the hero of Sir Walter Scott's novel. Clad in armour of steel inlaid with gold, and mounted on a gallant black horse, he rode into the lists and saluted the prince by lowering his lance.

10. Then he touched the shield of the most powerful of the challengers with the point of his lance, to indicate that he was ready to fight to the death. Shortly afterwards the two champions faced each other. The trumpets gave the signal; the horses rushed together; there was a shock like thunder. Both lances broke into fragments; the horses recoiled backwards on their haunches, but neither warrior fell. The spectators shouted, the ladies waved scarves and

handkerchiefs. Then all were silent as the warriors, armed with new lances, dashed together once more.

11. This time Ivanhoe was hit so fairly and squarely on the shield that he reeled in his saddle. He had, however, thrust his lance through the bars of his opponent's helmet, and horse and man rolled on the ground in a cloud of dust. The unhorsed knight sprang up and wished to fight with the sword on foot, but that was not allowed by the rules of the game. Loud were the shouts of delight at Ivanhoe's success.

12. The other challengers faced him, but each in turn fell before his lance, and the prize was awarded to him. It was a coronet of green satin with a circlet of gold around it. The prince placed it on the point of Ivanhoe's lance, and the conqueror rode along the front of the stand until he saw the lady of his choice. At her feet he placed the coronet, while the trumpets sounded and the heralds proclaimed her as the Queen of Beauty and of Love.

13. Tournaments were first held in England in Stephen's reign, and though discouraged by Henry the Second, they were revived by Richard the First "for the better training up of soldiers in feats of war, that they might grow more skilful and perfect in the same." The Church, however, set its face against them. Nevertheless, tournaments continued down to the middle of the sixteenth century, but long before this they had gone out of favour. They encouraged extravagance amongst the nobles, and frequently led to bloodshed. When gunpowder came into general use on the field of battle the day of the tournament passed away never to return.

21. KNIGHTHOOD.

1. In the last lesson we learnt how the knights disported themselves at the tournament. Who were these knights? You may often read in the newspapers a paragraph such as the following :—" After declaring the exhibition open, Mr. Henry Jones, chairman of the committee, was called forward to receive the honour of knighthood. Mr. Jones knelt before the King, and his Majesty, having borrowed a sword from an officer in attendance, placed it lightly on the shoulder of the worthy chairman and said, ' Rise, Sir Henry.'"

2. In our own days a knight is simply a man who has the right to use "Sir" as a prefix to his name. Knighthood is now an honour bestowed by the King on a person who has distinguished himself in some way. The knights of the Middle Ages, however, were members of a great brotherhood of soldiers. Most of them were of what is called " gentle birth," and they were supposed to follow those noble rules of life and conduct which we call chivalry.

3. True knights were expected to be courteous and kind to their equals and faithful to their superiors, to hate and shun falsehood, and to scorn meanness in any shape or form. They were also expected to be modest and generous, devout and pure, and never to see a wrong act done without trying to set it right. Above all, they were expected to be the champions of ladies in distress.

4. Of course, all knights did not live up to these high ideals, and most of them considered that they owed no duties at all to those who were in a lower rank of life than them-

THE VIGIL.

(From the picture by J. Pettie in the Tate Gallery.)

selves. Nevertheless knighthood was an excellent thing, for it did something to tame the roughest of warriors by holding before them as an example the figure of the perfect Christian knight. During the Crusades, when men's religious feelings were deeply touched, and during the Hundred Years' War, knighthood saw its best days.

5. At about twelve years of age the future knight became a page to some knight of renown. At fifteen or sixteen years of age he rose a step higher, and became a squire. He was now the companion of his lord, and most of his time was given to military exercises and manly sports. He learned to ride a battle-horse or charger, to wield sword, spear, and axe, to swim, to climb, to run and leap, to bear cold, heat, and thirst without complaining, and in all things to be a " very perfect gentle knight."

6. The squire bore the shield and armour of his lord to the field, and arrayed him for the fight. In battle his duty was to display the banner of his lord, to raise him from the ground when unhorsed, to supply him with his own horse in case of need, to rescue him if captured, to tend him if wounded, and to bury him honourably when dead.

7. After serving worthily as squire for six or seven years, the young man might ask to be made a knight. In time of war knights were usually " dubbed" on the eve of battle or after a victory. The squire simply knelt before the king, or some other knight of renown, and was tapped with a sword on the shoulder, while some such words as the following were said, " In the name of God, St. Michael, and St. George, I make thee knight. Be valiant, fearless, and loyal."

8. In times of peace knights were created with great pomp and ceremony. Nearly all the ceremonies were of a religious character. After bathing, which signified baptism, the young knight was clothed in a white tunic, which meant purity. Over that he donned a red robe, which reminded him of the blood he would have to shed, and over that again a black gown, which signified death. Then the new knight "watched his arms" in a church from sunset to sunrise, praying and fasting the while.

9. Finally he was presented to the person who was to knight him, and was "dubbed" as described above. Then the new knight went to prayers, and as he left the chapel the master-cook stopped him and said, "If you do anything contrary to the order of chivalry (which God forbid), I shall hack the spurs from your heels."

10. The Black Prince, the eldest son of Edward the Third, was a famous knight. You already know the story of how he won his spurs at Crécy. After the victory of Poictiers, when King John of France fell into his hands, he behaved like the true knight of romance.

11. He received the king with great respect, helped him off with his armour, and entertained him at supper along with the greater part of his princes and barons who had been taken prisoner. The Black Prince would not sit down with his royal guest, but served him with his own hands, declaring that "he was not worthy to sit at table with so great a king or so valiant a man." With such gracious words he did his best to make the French king forget the evil fortune of the day. When he entered London in triumph, on the twenty-fourth of May 1357, he mounted

King John on a fine white charger, and rode by his side on a little black hackney.

12. With all this show of knightly gentleness to his high-born captive, the Black Prince could be exceedingly cruel to helpless women and children. For example, when he captured the city of Limoges he ordered that no quarter should be given, and a terrible massacre took place of persons of all ranks and ages. This incident shows the great weakness of chivalry. It bound the knight to practise all sorts of courtesies towards men and women of his own rank, but all below he might treat with any degree of scorn and cruelty.

13. The chivalry which I have described in this lesson lasted from the beginning of the Crusades to the end of the Wars of the Roses, and then it passed away. Gunpowder came into use, and against gunpowder armour avails nothing. The kings no longer relied upon their armour-clad knights to win battles for them, and though the knights still kept up their tilts and tourneys, the day of their usefulness was over.

14. With the decay of the knight as a fighting man came the decay of chivalry. When armies began to fight on modern lines, there was no place for the knights of old. The whole spirit of knighthood made men "fight for their own hand," in order to win glory and renown for themselves, and not to unite with others in perfect discipline to win battles. Still, knighthood has left us as its legacy those ideals which remain as a guiding star to all who would "bear without abuse the grand old name of gentleman."

22. THE ASSIZES.

1. If you live in a large city or a county town, you will have noticed that every year judges come to your town to try law cases. Perhaps you have seen them. They are met at the station by the sheriff, who is usually a local landowner appointed by the king to see that justice is properly carried out in the county.

2. The judges are taken to their lodgings, and next day they go in state to church. They wear their robes and wigs, and they look very imposing indeed. The judge who is to try criminals wears a red gown, and the judge who is to try disputes between individuals wears a black gown. They ride in a state carriage, with men in the sheriff's livery on the box and standing up behind. As the judges enter the church the trumpeters blow a loud fanfare.

3. When service is over, the judges drive to the courts, where a guard of javelin men attends them. Then the assizes or sittings of the judges begin. When the trials are over, the judges move on to the next large town and hold courts there. You will notice that wherever they go the judges are treated with the greatest possible respect, because they come to do the king's work, and because they stand for justice, without which there could be no peace, or security, or happiness for anybody in the land.

4. Perhaps you will be surprised to know that this system of sending judges from one place to another throughout the kingdom is more than eight hundred years old. It was begun by Henry the First, and has gone on continuously

since the time of Henry the Second, the king who followed
Stephen on the throne. Henry the Second was a great
reformer. You remember how he tried to reform the
Church, but was opposed by Thomas Becket.

5. The dispute between the king and Becket was chiefly
concerned with a legal matter. Before Henry's time, clergymen who committed crimes were punished only in a bishops'
court, and the severest sentence that could be passed upon
them was to turn them out of the Church. This was a very
light punishment indeed for such grave crimes as murder
and robbery. Henry tried to do away with the bad custom,
but the Church was too strong for him. After Becket's
murder, Henry dared not propose to take away any of the
Church's privileges. He was, however, successful in bringing about other legal reforms.

6. In olden days the king was supposed to be the chief
judge of the kingdom. Our early kings used to travel
about the country and hold courts, at which any man who
complained that he could not get justice in the local courts
might have his case adjudged. When the kings gave up
this practice, judges were sent instead. In the terribly
disturbed reign of Stephen this plan fell through. Henry
the Second, however, revived it. He divided the country
into six " circuits," and sent judges to hold courts in them
so many times a year. These six circuits still remain, and to
them a seventh has been added—North and South Wales.

7. Now let us go inside the court. You see the judge
sitting at a desk on a raised platform beneath a canopy. On
his right sits the sheriff, and next to him is the chaplain.
On his left sit a body of twelve men, who are called

the jury, and these men have sworn on oath " to well and truly try" the cases brought before them. In front of the judge and to his right is the witness-box; and below him is a table, at which sit the clerks of the court, wearing gowns and wigs.

8. Facing the judge there is a row of desks, in which sit the barristers—that is, the highest class of lawyers. They also wear wigs and gowns. Behind them is the dock, in which the prisoner is placed; and behind the dock are seats for those members of the public who wish to be present at the trial.

9. A prisoner is brought into the dock by the jailers. The clerk of the court reads out the accusation against the prisoner, and then a barrister rises and gives the judge and jury a brief account of the crime which the prisoner is said to have committed. We will call this barrister the counsel for the crown or the prosecution.

10. When he has finished speaking, he calls his witnesses one by one. A man comes into the witness-box, and takes an oath on a copy of the New Testament, or swears with uplifted hand, that he will tell the truth, the whole truth, and nothing but the truth. Then the barrister begins to ask him questions, and the answers to the questions usually bear out the account which he has given of the crime. The judge takes notes of what the witness says.

11. When the barrister has asked a witness all his questions another barrister rises. He has been engaged to defend the prisoner, so we will call him the counsel for the defence. He, too, asks the witness a number of questions. He tries to show that the witness has made a mistake, or is not quite

First Trial by Jury.

(*From the cartoon by C. W. Cope, R.A.*)

sure of what he saw, or that what he said in answer to one question does not agree with what he said in answer to another, and so on. His business is to test the truth of what the witness says.

12. When all the witnesses against the prisoner have been examined and " cross-examined," the counsel for the defence calls witnesses in favour of the prisoner. These, too, are examined and cross-examined ; and all the while the judge takes notes. The prisoner himself may give evidence if he wishes to do so. When all the witnesses have been heard, the prisoner's counsel makes a speech showing that the prisoner is innocent, or that there is some doubt about the case, or that he ought to be treated mercifully.

13. Then the counsel for the crown makes another speech, drawing conclusions from the evidence which has been submitted, and showing that the prisoner ought to be found guilty. When he has finished speaking, the judge turns to the jury and " sums up." He points out to them the strong points and the weak points of the case in a very clear way, and explains to them the law on the subject. When he has done, he says, " You may now retire to consider your verdict."

14. The jurymen then leave the court and go into an adjoining room, where no one is allowed to come near them. There they discuss the case, and make up their minds whether the prisoner is guilty or innocent. When they have *all* agreed to a verdict, they come back into court. The clerk asks the foreman of the jury, " Do you find the prisoner guilty or not guilty ? "

15. If the verdict is " not guilty," the prisoner is at

once set free. If the verdict is "guilty," the judge asks the prisoner whether he has anything to say why sentence should not be pronounced. Sometimes the prisoner speaks; sometimes he does not. Then the judge gives sentence, and the sheriff's duty is to see that the sentence is properly carried out.

16. This is the way a trial by jury is carried on in English and Irish courts to-day. In Scotland it is not conducted in quite the same way. The chief points of difference between the English and Scottish practice in a trial of this kind are—(1) the witnesses do not swear an oath on a copy of the New Testament, but hold up the right hand and make a solemn statement; (2) in criminal cases there are fifteen jurymen, and not twelve as in England, and the verdict is given by a majority; and (3) a third verdict, that of "not proven," may be brought in if the jury think there is not sufficient evidence to convict the prisoner.

---

23. TRIAL BY JURY.

1. Now, when you were in court, I am sure you must have noticed one very important thing. It was not the judge who said whether the prisoner was guilty or not guilty; it was the jury. The "twelve good men and true" heard all that was said for and against the prisoner, and they decided his case.

2. These jurymen were twelve ordinary householders of the town. They were chosen from the list of voters; and when they were summoned to the court they were

bound to come, under a penalty of fine or imprisonment. If the prisoner thought that any of the jurymen would not deal justly with him, he could have had them sent away and others put in their places.

3. Now you see that the prisoner was tried, not by king or baron or judge, but by twelve of his fellow-countrymen. They all had to agree upon their verdict, and only when they said the terrible word " guilty " was the prisoner sentenced by the judge. This is called " trial by jury." Britons are very proud of this system ; they call it the " bulwark " of their liberties.

4. To find the beginnings of trial by jury, we must go back to the days of Henry the Second. The germ from which it grew was in existence before his time, but he was the first to establish it in such a way that it could grow into its modern form. In order to show you clearly what a great change Henry the Second brought about, let me give you an idea of a trial as it was conducted for more than a hundred years after the Norman Conquest.

5. Let us suppose the free landowners of the district have been called together to deal with the case of some man who is said to have committed a crime. They hear what is said for and against him, but they do not judge him. The judgment is left to Almighty God. The members of the court simply say how the man's guilt or innocence must be proved. They may, for example, say that the man who is charged with the crime must bring so many witnesses of a certain kind to swear solemnly that he is innocent. In those days men thought that he who swore falsely would suffer some swift and terrible punish-

ment : he would be struck dead, or turned into a dwarf, or would suffer some other horrible fate.

6. If the accused man brought the right number and the right kind of witnesses to swear for him, he was allowed to go free. Usually, however, after the Norman Conquest, the court thought that oaths were not sufficient. In such a case, it sent a prisoner to the "ordeal"—that is, he had to undergo the judgment of fire or water. In the case of the ordeal by water, the priest called upon the water to receive the innocent man and reject the guilty. Then the man was thrown into the water. If he sank, he was innocent ; if he floated, he was guilty. Sometimes the man was drowned by the time he had proved himself innocent.

7. If the ordeal was by fire, the prisoner was ordered to take up a piece of red-hot iron, one pound in weight, and carry it three paces. His hand was then bound up and sealed. Three days later the seal was broken, and the hand was examined by the priest. If the wound had healed sufficiently, the prisoner was innocent ; if it showed a blister "as large as half a walnut," he was guilty. You can easily see how uncertain this kind of judgment was, and how it lent itself to fraud on the part of the priests and others who conducted the trials.

8. The Normans brought with them another kind of ordeal, the ordeal by combat—that is, an appeal to the God of battles. The accuser and the accused, if they were not maimed, or too young or too old, had to fight with each other, and the one who was victor was considered to have God on his side. The fight was carried out with special

arms made of wood and horn, and the combat might continue from dawn to twilight.

9. The object of each party was not to kill his adversary but to make him cry "Craven," in which case he was adjudged guilty, and was forthwith hanged or mutilated or fined according to the character of his crime. Thus you see that the stronger and more skilful man had a good chance of getting judgment in his favour, even though he were guilty of the crime laid to his charge.

10. Now the Norman kings always considered that they could, if they wished, have disputes as to *land* settled without trial by ordeal. They sometimes gave orders to their officers to call together the men of the neighbourhood, and make them swear an oath to say truly to whom the land in dispute belonged. The ownership of the land was then decided according to the oaths of these men.

11. The great change which Henry the Second brought about was to give all his subjects the right to have their disputes settled in this way, if they so wished. In course of time this "inquest," as it was called, took the place of the old plan, not only with regard to land, but also with regard to murder and robbery and other crimes.

12. Now notice that the neighbours who were called together were rather witnesses than judges. They decided the case on their own knowledge, and in this respect they were quite different from the jurymen of to-day, who are judges and not witnesses. Our jurymen are supposed to know nothing about the case until they come into the court, and they are required to "give their verdict" simply and solely on what they hear from the witnesses. Frequently they are

warned to take no notice of what they have read in the newspapers about the case.

13. You can easily see that the jury of King Henry's day might do great injustice to a man brought before them. They must often have decided their cases by guess-work and by the tittle-tattle of the countryside. No doubt many a man was hanged, not because any one had seen him commit a crime, but because he had a bad name amongst his neighbours, and was just the kind of man they would expect to do such a deed. The old proverb, " Give a dog a bad name, and hang him," must have applied to many men also.

14. In course of time the judges began to insist that the jurymen must listen to what the witnesses said, and give their verdict, not of their own knowledge, but according to the evidence. Many generations, however, went by before the rule was laid down that " hearsay is no evidence," and trial by jury took its modern form.

---

24. THE GREAT CHARTER.

1. To-day we will in imagination take a walk by the side of the river Thames. We will set out from the quaint old town of Staines, which takes its name from the " London Stone," set up in the year 1280 to mark the boundary of Middlesex. We cross the bridge, and follow the river up-stream for about a mile until we come to a meadow now used as Egham racecourse. Opposite to it is a small island. Perhaps you will say, " I see nothing remarkable about this

meadow and island." Quite true, but nowhere in England can we find a place of greater historical importance.

2. The meadow is called Runnymede, and the island opposite to it is known as Magna Charta Island. Magna Charta, or Carta, means the " Great Charter ; " and a charter is a legal document setting forth the rights and privileges

MAGNA CHARTA ISLAND.

of a people or of a corporation — that is, of a body of men who in law are treated as if they were one person. Here, on this meadow, the Great Charter, which has been called the "keystone of English liberty," was signed by King John in the year 1215. John, you will remember, was the seventh of our Norman kings. He succeeded that great warrior and Crusader, Richard the First.

3. John was the youngest and best beloved son of Henry the Second. He was a bad boy and a bad man, and when he became king he was the worst monarch who ever sat on the English throne. You already know that he murdered his nephew Arthur. There was no wickedness too bad for him. He was cruel, false, greedy, untruthful, and vile; yet out of his wickedness came the beginning of the liberties in which we rejoice to-day.

4. John had not been long on the throne before he lost nearly all the wide possessions in France over which Henry the Second had ruled. This was a great blessing to England. Formerly the Norman knights spent half their time abroad, and looked upon Normandy as their real home. When Normandy was lost, they were compelled to give all their attention to England. As time went on they became Englishmen, and were proud of the country which they had formerly despised. The great-grandsons of the men who fought on opposite sides at Hastings became friends and brothers, and thus grew up the " new English race."

5. John had not been long on the throne before he began to quarrel with the Church. The Pope at that time was Innocent the Third, a bold, arrogant man, who meant to make the Church supreme in every Christian land. Formerly, when an archbishop was to be chosen, the king named the man for the post, and the Pope and the clergy accepted him. In 1205, when the Archbishop of Canterbury died, the clergy chose a new archbishop for themselves without asking the king's permission. This made John very angry indeed.

6. He forced the clergy to chose a favourite of his own; but the Pope would have neither the king's favourite nor the man chosen by the clergy. He himself chose as arch-bishop a scholar named Stephen Langton, who was a wise and pious Englishman. No better choice could have been made. John, however, refused to let Langton come to England, and soon a fierce quarrel began between the king and the Pope. Innocent was just as masterful a man as John, and the quarrel became a trial of strength between them.

7. The Pope laid an interdict on the realm—that is, he cut off England from the Church altogether. The churches and churchyards were closed; the church bells never rang, and the dead were buried in fields and by the roadside. The clergy stood by the Pope, but still John would not yield. He seized the estates of the bishops, and punished the clergy whenever he could.

8. At last the Pope deposed the king, and gave his kingdom to Philip of France, who at once began to prepare a fleet and an army to invade England. The English barons and people were quite ready to fight the French king, but King John was now thoroughly frightened. He begged forgiveness of the Pope; he knelt before the Pope's messenger, and gave up his kingdom to him. Then he received it back as the vassal of the Pope. The anger of the English people at this base act knew no bounds. "He has become the Pope's man," they said; "he is no longer a king, but a slave." Still more angry did they become when John took an army to France and was hopelessly beaten.

King John Signing Magna Charta.

(*From the fresco by Ernest Normand in the Royal Exchange, London.*)

9. Many of the barons had refused to follow the king to France, and on his return he began to punish them. This was the last straw that broke down their patience. The barons now banded together under Stephen Langton, the Archbishop of Canterbury, who showed them the Charter which Henry the First had given to the people one hundred years before. The barons bound themselves to make the king put his seal to a similar charter, even if they had to fight him to do so. They girded on their armour, and under Robert Fitzwalter, " the marshal of the army of God and the holy Church," marched to London, where the citizens threw open the gates to receive them. All the king's knights but seven left him, and then he saw that he must give way.

10. Now look at the picture on page 123. It represents the great scene that took place on Magna Charta Island on June 15, 1215. You see in the background a great tent, with banners waving above it. In front of the tent is a throne, with the lions of England embroidered on it. Sitting on the throne is King John, with the sword of state in his hand. There is a scowl on his face, but he is trying hard not to show his anger. When he gets home to-night he will fling himself on the ground, gnash his teeth, and in a passion of rage curse the Charter which he has been forced to sign.

11. Around the king on all sides are barons in full armour. Look at their faces. They are stern and strong. The barons have suffered much from the king; now they are determined that he shall make the law and keep it. A monk is reading the Charter, but the king is not listening. He is planning

No free man shall be taken, or imprisoned, or dispossessed, or outlawed,

or banished, or in any way destroyed, nor will we go upon him nor upon

him send, except by the legal judgment of his peers or by the law of the land.

To no one will we sell, to no one will we deny or delay, right or justice.

SECTIONS 39 AND 40 OF MAGNA CHARTA.

revenge on the barons. By the king's side is the Pope's legate, to whom John has surrendered his kingdom. You see from the look on his face that he hates the Charter, and thinks John ought not to be forced to sign it. John, however, cannot help himself. When the reading is finished he says, "Let it be sealed." Then the Charter is placed on the table in front of him, the wax is melted and placed on the parchment, the seal is screwed down, and Magna Charta becomes for all time the LAW.

12. Now what is the meaning of this Charter which has just been sealed? It is really a treaty of peace between the king and his people. "We will retain you as king," they say, "only on condition that you will swear to keep the law as it is written down on this parchment." Now, from what source did they get this law? It was not entirely a new thing, for it included the old rights and the old liberties of the people collected together and put into writing. The

Houses of Parliament.

Parliament was first called to Westminster by Edward the First, and there it has continued to sit till the present time. The Houses of Parliament were burned down in October 1834, and of the ancient buildings Westminster Hall and the crypt of St. Stephen's alone were

Charter of Henry the First which Langton had shown the barons was the ground-work of part of the new Charter. But Henry's Charter itself was not new; it was based on the laws of Edward the Confessor, which, in turn, were based on still older laws.

13. All the freemen of the land had banded together to force the king to sign the Charter, and the rights of all classes of the people are laid down in it. Much of the Charter deals with the rights of the barons and the clergy, but one-third of it contains promises and guarantees for the people in general. The barons, unlike those of some foreign countries, were not selfish when they gained the upper hand of the king. It is true that they took good care of themselves, but they did not forget the welfare of the nation at large.

14. Ever since the days of King John, the Great Charter has been part of the written law of our land. Whenever kings in after times did unlawful and tyrannical things, the people forced them to swear to keep the Great Charter. It has been signed nearly forty times.

15. I cannot now tell you all the rights which were guaranteed to the English people by this Charter. The three chief things to remember are that—(1) The people could only be taxed with the consent of the king's council; (2) there must be justice for all, and justice must not be sold, refused, or delayed; (3) no freeman could be taken, imprisoned, or in any way hurt, unless he be tried by his peers or equals according to the law. Somewhat changed in form, these principles are still the foundation stones of our law.

25. THE HOUSE OF COMMONS.

1. To-day we will pay a visit to the Houses of Parliament. We must make our way to that part of London known as Westminster. In early days it was a marshy island in the Thames, and on it Edward the Confessor built a palace and a great church. Where the palace stood, the Houses of Parliament now stand ; where the church was built, the abbey of Westminster may now be seen.

2. We cross New Palace Yard, and enter a door guarded by a policeman. We are now in Westminster Hall, and we gaze at its ancient walls and the blackened beams of its great oak roof with much interest. We may well do so, for this hall has been the scene of some of the greatest events in the story of our land. It was built by William Rufus between the years 1097 and 1099, and was rebuilt by Richard the Second some three hundred years later.

3. Some of our earliest Parliaments met in it, and it was the seat of the chief law courts of the country down to the year 1880, when the new Courts in the Strand were opened. A king and several ministers of state have received their death sentences in this hall. If its ancient walls could speak, they would tell us more of English history than even the most learned men know.

4. We now pass on to St. Stephen's Hall, with its vaulted roof, rich carving, and many statues. From this place we are taken up a stone staircase, up and up, until we come to what is called the Strangers' Gallery. From this gallery we look down upon the House of Commons. " Not much to see," perhaps you say. Certainly the House itself is a

small and very plain hall, yet it is by far the most important place in the land.

5. Looking down from the gallery we see a broad gang-way. At one end of it there is a kind of throne with a table in front of it. On the throne sits a figure in a flowing silk gown and a great white wig. This is the Speaker or Chairman of the House. On the table in front of him you see a gold staff with a heavy head shaped like a crown. This is the mace. It is carried before the Speaker, and it rests upon the table all the time that he occupies the chair. When he leaves the chair, and the chairman of committees takes his place, the mace is put on supports under the ledge of the table.

6. On each side of the gangway there is an array of benches covered with green leather. On the Speaker's right hand sit those members of Parliament who support the Government ; on his left hand sit those who oppose it. The front benches on either side are reserved for the leaders of the two great parties in the House. On the Treasury Bench, which is the front bench on the right hand of the Speaker, you see members of the Government.

7. There are six hundred and seventy members of Parlia-ment altogether, but there is not room for anything like that number to sit down. When great events are taking place many members have to stand. In a gallery right opposite to you are the reporters, busy taking down the speeches which are being delivered. Above the Reporters' Gallery is the Ladies' Gallery, which is shut in by a grille or grating.

8. I am afraid that you will soon be tired of sitting in the gallery. You see the members rise one after another,

and hear them make long, sometimes very long, speeches. Now I am sure that you can understand the meaning of the word *Parliament*. It is an old French word, and it means a place for speaking.

9. Nobody seems to pay much attention to the majority of the speakers, but now and then one of the leaders sitting on the front benches has something to say. Then those behind him cry " Hear, hear," to express their approval of what he says, while the members on the other side shout " No, no," or in other ways show that they disagree with him. Then, perhaps, the members all troop out into the lobbies to give their vote on the question which they have been debating.

10. Now what is the work that the members of the House of Commons do day by day ? They help to make the laws of the land, or to amend them when necessary ; they decide what money we shall pay to the king's officers to keep up the government of the country ; they ventilate our grievances ; they keep a close watch over the acts of the Government ; and they are zealous to preserve our liberties.

11. Together with the House of Lords, they are the greatest power in the land—higher even than the king. These two Houses make the laws, and when the king signs them they are put in force. Not a single farthing of money may be taken from the people without the consent of the House of Commons. It holds the purse-strings of the nation, and no one may loosen them unless the majority of the members agree.

12. Perhaps you ask, " Who gives the members of the

The Mace—the symbol of the dignity and privileges of the House of Commons.

St. Stephen's Hall, occupying the site of the old St. Stephen's Chapel.

———

The House of Lords, sometimes known as The Gilded Chamber.

The House of Commons. On the right of the Speaker's Chair are the Government Benches; to the left are the Opposition Benches. Above the Speaker's Chair is the Press Gallery; and above that the Grille, behind which ladies sit.

THE HOUSES OF PARLIAMENT.

House of Commons the right to go to Parliament and to do these things?" The answer is very simple. The British people choose their members at what is called a parliamentary election. Most of the men-householders and many of the lodgers in this country have the right to choose the member of Parliament who is to speak for them. When your father gives his vote at election times, he is really helping to rule his country ; he is choosing the man who is to do his work for him. Nearly every grown-up Briton is thus a partner in the work of government.

13. You must not imagine that this has always been so. In earlier days the government was in the hands of kings and nobles, who made what laws they pleased, and took from the people what money they wanted. The people are now all-powerful, but in those days they were of no account at all. Their rights have been won for them by the long and bitter struggles of their forefathers. A fierce war was waged and a king lost his head before the power was taken from the few and given to the many. In the next lesson I shall tell you something about the beginnings of Parliament.

---

26. THE BEGINNINGS OF PARLIAMENT.

1. For the beginnings of Parliament we must go back to the days of Henry the Third, the son of wicked King John. Henry the Third was a boy of nine when his father died. There was no crown with which to crown him; it had been lost with much of John's baggage in the quicksands of the Wash. A plain circlet of gold was placed on the lad's

head, and he was made king of a kingdom full of strife and misery.

2. Happily there were two strong barons who ruled in the name of the king, and they soon brought about peace to the land. One of these was William the Marshal, and the other was Hubert de Burgh, of whom you read in Book III. Under these men Prince Lewis of France, who had been offered the crown by the barons, and had landed with an army in order to seize it, was defeated both by land and sea, and was forced to retire to France.

3. Henry began to rule in his own name in the year 1227. He soon showed himself jealous of Hubert de Burgh, who had become regent on the death of the Earl-Marshal, and had proved a tower of strength to the kingdom. Hubert was driven from his office, and then Henry gave himself up to bad advisers. Smooth-tongued, flattering foreigners were more to his liking than blunt, honest Englishmen. So he brought over many Frenchmen, and lavished money, earldoms, and bishoprics upon them.

4. Henry's love of foreign favourites, and the very heavy burdens which he laid upon England at the demand of the Pope, at last roused the barons. They met together, and told the young king that his foreign favourites were eating up the land like a flight of locusts. They also said that he could not be allowed to rule any longer without the aid and counsel of his barons.

5. Now the leader of the barons was the best and bravest man of his time. He was Simon de Montfort, Earl of Leicester. Strange to say, he too was a foreigner, and had been brought over from France as one of the king's

favourites. He had married the king's sister, and had
become to all intents and purposes an Englishman. He
was a truly great man, strong and bold, pious, wise, and
honourable. After he died, the people worshipped him as
a saint. They called him St. Simon the Righteous, and
believed that miracles were wrought at his shrine.

6. With the barons at his back, Simon forced the king
to swear that he would keep the law as laid down in Magna
Charta. This Henry did time after time, but he did not keep
his promises. He once swore to keep faith as " a man, a
Christian, a knight, a crowned and anointed king ; " but he
broke this oath just as lightly as he had broken the rest.
Soon the barons saw that they could place no reliance on
his word, and that they would have to use force to make
him observe his promises.

7. They met in full armour at Oxford in the year 1258,
and there the king had to agree to their terms. A special
Council of fifteen bishops and barons was appointed to rule
the land in the name of the king. In this way the government of the land was taken altogether out of the hands of
the king and given to a sort of committee.

8. This went on for four years ; but there was trouble all
the time, for the barons soon became jealous of each other.
Many of them went over to the king, who had been freed
from his oath by the Pope. At length, in 1264, he got
together an army, and a battle was fought at Lewes ; the
king's men were overthrown, and he himself was taken
prisoner. Then Earl Simon became the real ruler of
England.

9. In the next year Earl Simon called together a Parlia-

ment in the king's name.   This Parliament is very famous, because it was the beginning of Parliament as we know it to-day.   Up to this time the king's Council was the only body which came together to help in ruling the country. It was composed of archbishops, bishops, abbots, earls, barons, and smaller landholders or squires, and they alone had the right to come to the Council and give advice to the king.

10. Now in those days it was very difficult to get from one part of the country to another.   We can go from London to Edinburgh in about eight hours, but six hundred years ago a man would take weeks to accomplish the journey.   The roads were few and bad, there were all sorts of dangers by the way, and the cost was very great.   For this and other reasons the country squires never used their right of coming to the king's Council as a body.

11. But what of the common people ?   They had no part or lot in the Great Council at all.   Only those who owned land were allowed to have a voice in governing the country.   Earl Simon, however, wished all classes to take part in Parliament ; so he called together not only nobles, bishops, abbots, and squires, but also *two townsmen to be chosen by each town*.   Because Simon's Parliament had in it representatives of all classes of freemen in the land, it is often called the first English Parliament.   It met in the year 1265.

12. The archbishops, bishops, abbots, great nobles, squires, and townsmen all sat in one chamber.   Not until the early years of Edward the Third's reign was Parliament divided into the two Houses—the House of Lords and the House of

Commons—as we have them to-day. In the House of Lords sit nobles, who speak only for themselves ; in the House of Commons sit the men who speak for the people of the shires and the towns.

13. Simon's Parliament was not remarkable for anything that it did, but because, for the first time, it brought representatives of the towns to the Great Council of the nation, and united lords, county members, and borough members into one Parliament. After Simon's death, which took place at the battle of Evesham, in 1265, no Parliament on this model was called for thirty years. In the year 1295, however, Edward the First brought together a Parliament which historians consider to be the real ancestor of the Parliament of to-day.

27. THE MONASTERIES.

1. Come with me to the old town of Chepstow, which stands near the mouth of the beautiful river Wye, in the border county of Monmouth. We have not come to examine the town itself, nor the old castle which in the twelfth century belonged to Strongbow, the famous knight who paved the way for the conquest of Ireland. We are going to row up the river for some ten miles or so, to visit one of the most beautiful ruins in England.

2. With the tide in our favour, we ply our oars and make rapid progress along the great bends of the much-winding river, with its wooded cliffs rising high on either hand. At length we see before us, on the right bank of the stream, the far-famed ruins of Tintern Abbey, a monastery,

or abode of monks, which was founded as far back as the days of King Henry the First. The ruins stand close to the river in a most romantic valley. You will scarcely find a more picturesque spot in all England.

3. The monks who lived in this monastery were men who had withdrawn themselves from the world in order to live a life of prayer, fasting, and good works. In the twelfth century monasteries filled with monks were found in all parts of England, usually in retired and beautiful places near to a river or stream, which provided them with fish for the fasting-days.

4. The monks belonged to one or other of the "orders" or brotherhoods, the chief and oldest of which was the Benedictine order, founded by St. Benedict, who lived in the sixth century, and drew up the rules which the monks who joined him had to obey.

5. A Benedictine monk had to renounce the world, the flesh, and the devil, and to give up to the monastery all the property which he possessed. Once a monk, he was always a monk, and in the eyes of the law he became as one dead. He had to bind himself to obey his superior in all things. His time was not his own, for every hour of the day and night was allotted to religious exercises, or to work, study, sleep, or recreation.

6. All the monks were dressed alike, in undyed garments; all slept in the same chamber, or dormitory; all took their meals together in a dining-hall, or refectory; all attended at least seven services in the church each day and night; and all met regularly in their chapter-house to discuss matters of business and discipline. A monk who was

negligent or disobedient was severely punished ; and no one might go outside the bounds without permission.

7. For several centuries the Benedictines strictly obeyed the rules of their order, and lived holy and useful lives. Then they began to fall away from their high standard, and to become idle and careless and fond of luxury. Reformers arose who founded new " orders," with the object of bringing back the monks to their old strictness of life. One of these reformers appeared in Burgundy in the year 1020, and founded the brotherhood afterwards known as the Cistercians. In 1128 the Cistercians built their first abbey in Surrey. Tintern was the third religious house which they established in this country.

8. At first the " rule " of the Cistercians was very strict indeed. They wore no boots, gloves, shirts, or cowls to protect them from the weather. From Easter to September they had only one meal a day. As a general rule they had to keep silence, and if they spoke they had to acknowledge their fault in the chapter-house and do penance for it. Their buildings, unlike those of the other " orders," were not lavishly adorned. In later times some of the strictest rules were broken, but even now we can tell a Cistercian abbey by the grace and simplicity of its buildings.

9. Now, as we stand gazing at the wonderful ruin of Tintern, let us try to picture it as it was in the days of its glory. Here is a plan that will help us. You see at once that the most important part of the monastery was the church, which was built in the form of a cross. Even in its ruins we cannot help admiring the soaring pillars, the fine arches, and the beautiful tracery of the windows.

10. To the north of the nave was a green lawn known as the cloister-garth, which formed, as it were, the courtyard of the monastery. Round it were the cloisters, or covered-in walks, from which access was obtained to all parts of the buildings. The cloister was the place of business, the

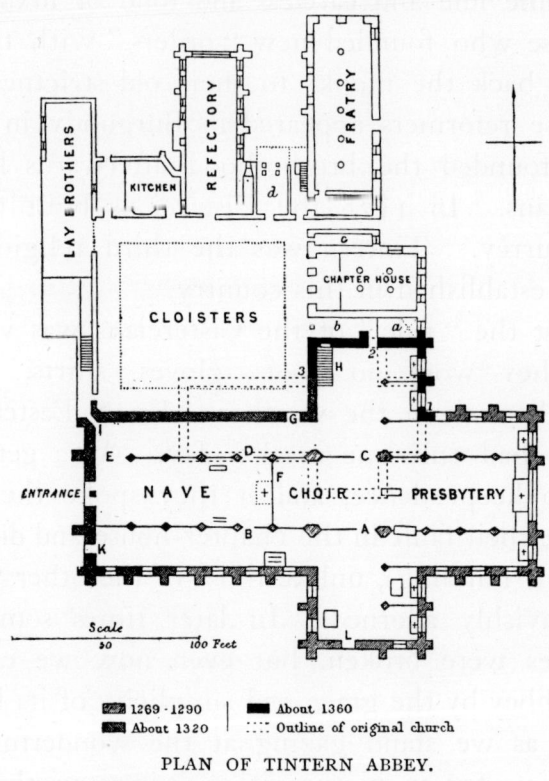

PLAN OF TINTERN ABBEY.

study, and the common workshop. Here the books were read and the indoor work was done. In most monasteries the cloisters were on the south or sunny side; but at Tintern they were on the north side, because it was secluded and nearer to the river.

11. On the east side of the cloister-garth was the chapter-house, where the monks met their abbot daily ; and adjoining the chapter-house was a parlour, so called because the monks at certain times were allowed to visit it in order to speak with their relatives. Near at hand, too, was the infirmary, in which the sick monks were tended, and also those who had grown too old and feeble to live the hard life of their " order."

12. To the north of the chapter-house was the day room of the monks, above which was the dormitory, in which they all slept together. A long passage and a flight of steps enabled them to go directly from the dormitory to the church during the night. Over the chapter-house was the scriptorium, in which the monks made copies of sacred and other books, and adorned them with gold and rich colouring in many a quaint and beautiful design.

13. To the north of the cloister-garth was the refectory, or dining-hall. Near the entrance were troughs of water, at which the monks washed their hands before going into the hall. The monks sat at tables and kept silence during the meals, while a reader in a pulpit read out passages of Scripture or of some religious book. The food was passed from the kitchen to the hall through a hatch. A doorway from the kitchen led to the house of the lay brothers. These were the business men of the monastery. Some of them managed the farms belonging to the monastery, and lived at the granges, or farmhouses. In or near the quarters of the lay brethren the guests who sought lodging and food at the monastery were received.

14. The monasteries in their best days did a noble work

for the country. The monks were the only body of learned men in the land. They were famous builders, and understood carpentry, smith's work, and jeweller's work. They wrote and copied books ; they studied the arts of drawing and painting and music ; they were excellent farmers, and planted beautiful gardens.

15. They were the friends of the poor, and helped them in times of sickness and distress. No stranger was ever turned away from their gates ; food and lodging and medical attendance were provided for all who sought them. What the workhouse and the hospital now do for the poor, the monasteries did for them in the Middle Ages.

16. Kings, noblemen, and rich men constantly gave lands and money to the monasteries, and in time they became very wealthy. Some of the monasteries possessed great farms with immense flocks of sheep, while others had extensive iron-works. Many of the monasteries were great employers of labour, and had large numbers of carpenters, millers, masons, fishermen, and husbandmen in their pay. As the monks grew more and more wealthy, they began to live in plenty and careless ease, and sometimes in actual wickedness.

17. The monasteries did their chief work in the country districts. Meanwhile towns and cities had grown greatly. The freemen of the towns lived in comfort and security, but within the crowded courts, outside the walls, and in the marshes by the rivers, crowds of men and women herded in filth and wretchedness. Amongst them were the lepers, the victims of that foul disease which had been brought from the East by the Crusaders. The monks did little or nothing for these poor creatures.

18. In the first quarter of the thirteenth century the "begging" friars came to England with a ministry of love and hope to the poor and the outcast. The first to come were the Franciscans—that is, the followers of St. Francis. They were the apostles of poverty. They went forth to heal the sick and cleanse the leper, providing neither gold nor silver in their purses, neither two coats, neither shoes nor yet staves. They preached the half-forgotten gospel to the wretched and vile, and ministered to their bodily needs as well. They set up their houses, not in pleasant country places by gently-flowing streams, but amidst the hovels of the poor. Their chief settlement in England was in Newgate, London, in a spot called Stinking Lane.

19. St. Francis wished his followers to be simple, unlettered men; but in the course of time they studied medicine, so as to be better able to cope with disease. Thus they became the chief doctors of the Middle Ages. The famous Roger Bacon was a Franciscan, and he is generally held to be the father of modern science. There were many other famous Franciscans, and some of them became the chief teachers at the universities.

---

28. THE STORY OF WALES.—I.

1. Come with me to the seaside town of Rhyl, on the Flintshire coast of North Wales. It is neither a picturesque nor an ancient town, but it possesses magnificent sands, on which crowds of happy holiday-makers disport themselves every summer. You and I, however, have not come to

Rhyl to bathe, to ride donkeys, or to build sand-castles. We have come to make it the starting-point for a little historical excursion up the beautiful Vale of Clwyd, which is shut in on the east, south, and west by lofty peaked mountains.

2. We leave Rhyl by the bridge which crosses the railway at the east end of the station, and keep straight on over Morfa Rhuddlan—"the Marsh of Rhuddlan"—for two and a half miles. Then we turn sharp to the right and soon reach the village. Presently we halt before the end wall of a row of cottages and see a stone with the following inscription : "*This fragment is the remains of the building where King Edward the First held his Parliament, A.D. 1283, in which was passed the Statute of Rhuddlan, securing to the Principality of Wales its judicial rights and independence.*"

3. Close by we see the ruins of the massive castle of Rhuddlan, with its ivied walls seventeen feet thick, and its great towers at each corner and at the entrance gates. This great Welsh stronghold was founded early in the tenth century. It was captured by Edward the First, who rebuilt it in the year 1277. Now here we are face to face with historic remains which speak forcibly to us of the days when Wales was just conquered by the English king who first made a serious attempt to unite all parts of Britain under one ruler. No place is more suitable in which to recall the story of " gallant little Wales."

4. The people of Wales, as you already know, are the descendants of the natives or Celts whom the Romans found inhabiting the whole island of Britain when they came to conquer it. These Celts consisted of many tribes, but they

WHERE THE STATUTE OF RHUDDLAN WAS PASSED.

all belonged to two great branches—the Cymry in the southern part of Britain, and the Gaels in the Highlands of Scotland and in Ireland. To this day the Celts retain their old language. It is still spoken in Wales, in Ireland, and in the Highlands of Scotland. To this day the dalesmen of Cumberland count their sheep in Welsh.

5. If you study a map of Wales, you will see that its mountains not only form a barricade against England, but also prevent easy communication between the different parts of the country. Wales can be entered from England only by three valleys—namely, along the Dee, the Severn, and the Wye. To get from North to South Wales is equally difficult. Suppose, for example, that you wish to travel by railway from Carmarthen, in South Wales, to

Carnarvon, in North Wales. Two routes, and two routes only, are open to you. You may travel to the English border, proceed northward to Chester, and then skirt the coast of North Wales until you reach your destination. Or you may travel to the shores of Cardigan Bay at Aberystwith, and then follow the coastline nearly all the way to Carnarvon.

6. If the routes are so roundabout in our time, what must they have been in the days before highroads and railways? Now I think you can understand how the mountains kept out the English who tried to conquer the land, and how they also prevented the Welsh from uniting into one strong nation.

7. Up to the close of the sixth century the British remained masters of all the western part of the island from the Clyde to Exeter. In the year 577 A.D. the English gained a great victory at Deorham in Gloucestershire, and won for themselves the great plain of the Severn. They thus thrust a wedge between the Britons south of the Bristol Channel and those north of that estuary.

8. Thirty-six years later a Northumbrian king fought a host of Welsh princes beneath the walls of the old Roman city of Chester. The English were victorious, and they occupied the plain from which the walls and towers of the city arose. In this way they thrust a wedge between the Britons south of the Dee and the Britons north of it.

9. Wales was thus cut off from Strathclyde on the north and from West Wales or Cornwall on the south. It was surrounded on the land side by a fierce people who spoke a strange language and worshipped strange gods, for the

English were heathen and the Welsh were Christian. It was also open to attack from the sea. The Danes made frequent descents, and at length settled on the south coast, where they discovered and named Milford and other havens, and founded the town of Tenby. Only by constant fighting could the swarming enemy be kept at bay.

10. From the year 844 to 877 a king named Rhodri or Roderick Mawr—that is, "the Great"—drove back the Danes and played the part of King Alfred in Wales. Rhodri fell in battle against the English in 877, and the land was in a sad condition until the great King Llywelyn ap Seisyll arose. The princes acknowledged him as overlord, and he became chief king of all Wales. He cleared the land of Dane and English, and at his death in 1027 Wales was a prosperous and happy country.

---

29. THE STORY OF WALES.—II.

1. When Llywelyn died, the princes said that they would not obey another over-king, and a time of great bloodshed and misery followed. Then Griffith, the son of Llywelyn, took up his father's work. He beat the English, he crushed those princes who opposed the unity of Wales, and he defeated the sea-rovers. Just at this time Earl Harold, afterwards King of England, invaded Wales. Owing to his good generalship and to the treachery of the Welsh princes who were jealous of Griffith, Harold was successful. Griffith, who had been "the head and shield of the Britons," was slain by traitors amongst his own men.

SOME FAMOUS WELSH CASTLES.

1. Pembroke. 2. Carnarvon. 3. Harlech. 4. Conway. 5. Caerphilly. 6. Rhuddlan.
7. Kidwelly. 8. Denbigh : the keep.

2. In January 1070, when William the Conqueror had established himself in England, he attempted the invasion of Wales. While the snow lay thick on the mountains he appeared at Chester, but was unable to advance any further. He turned back, but he placed on the borders a number of barons, whose duty it was to conquer the country.

3. Hugh the Wolf, from whom the present Duke of Westminster is descended, was placed at Chester ; Robert, his nephew, was made Lord of Clwyd, and went to and fro from his castle at Rhuddlan butchering the Welsh without mercy. Norman barons were also placed at Shrewsbury, Hereford, and other places. Meanwhile, the Welsh chiefs were fighting amongst themselves. In 1081 the Conqueror again took the field, seized Cardiff, and built its castle. Wales looked as though it would soon be entirely conquered by the Normans.

4. In this dark hour two famous princes arose to lead the Welsh against the invader. They were Griffith ap Conon, Prince of North Wales, and Griffith ap Rees, his son, Prince of South Wales. Rees was an abler and more powerful man than his father, and he won a memorable victory at Cardigan in 1136 against the strongest army which the Normans could put into the field.

5. When Henry the Second came to the throne, he found two strong Welsh princes, Owen Gwynedd in North Wales and the Lord Rees in South Wales. These men were about to become allies, and thus bring about the union of Wales. To prevent this, Henry invaded the country three times with great armies ; but the storms and the

mountains fought against him, and he was obliged to leave Wales unconquered.

6. Owen Gwynedd died in 1170, and once more the chiefs quarrelled and refused to unite. Twenty-four years later, however, we find Llywelyn the Great, the grandson of Owen Gwynedd, becoming powerful. His reign was in many respects the most important in Welsh history. He encouraged the bard, the monk, and the friar, and he laboured hard for peace and unity.

7. The Wales over which Llywelyn ruled consisted of Anglesey and the country to the west of the Snowdon, Berwyn, and Plinlimmon ranges. He allied himself with the barons who were opposing King John, and his rights are specially preserved in Magna Charta. Llywelyn deserved his title "The Great," for he was the best of all the native rulers of Wales.

8. We are now rapidly drawing near to the last scene in the story of Wales as an independent nation. The "last Llywelyn" was the grandson of Llywelyn the Great. At first he ruled jointly with his brothers, Owen and David, but by 1255 he was sole ruler of all Wales. He strove hard to extend his sway, and in 1267 he ruled the land from Snowdon to the Dee, and as far south as the Towy and the Brecknockshire Beacons—that is, he was master of nearly all modern Wales, with the exception of the seaboard and the shores of the Bristol Channel.

9. When the barons under Simon de Montfort took up arms against Henry the Third, Llywelyn joined them. Many of the Welsh barons, however, joined the king and invaded Llywelyn's dominions, which soon shrank to their

old limits. Edward the First became King of England in 1272, and then began a long struggle which ended in the downfall of Wales. He first ordered Llywelyn to do homage for his country, and this command Llywelyn refused to obey.

10. In 1282 Edward's great army began to close round the vast mountain mass of Snowdon in which Llywelyn lay. Winter was coming on, and Edward was thinking of retiring and waiting until the next year, when news arrived that Llywelyn was slain. He had left Snowdon and gone to South Wales in order to encourage the chiefs in their resistance to Edward. In a slight skirmish near Builth a soldier slew him, not knowing who he was. When the men of Snowdon learned that their prince had fallen they lost heart. Their cause was now hopeless, and in a few months the whole of Wales was at Edward's feet.

11. In 1284 Edward called the chiefs together at Rhuddlan and passed the Statute of Wales, which, as the inscription on the wall tells us, secured to the principality "its judicial rights and independence." Llywelyn's realm was then divided into six shires—Carnarvon, Anglesey, Merioneth, Flint, Cardigan, and Carmarthen—and was governed in the same way as the English counties. Much, however, of the old Welsh law remained.

12. The king's sheriffs took the place of the Welsh chieftains, and Edward's eldest son, afterwards Edward the Second, was created Prince of Wales. From that day to this the title Prince of Wales has been conferred by the King of England on his eldest son. The present Prince of Wales has another claim on the loyalty of the Welsh people—he is actually descended from a daughter of Llywelyn the Great.

30. THE CORONATION STONE.

1. Across the road from the Houses of Parliament is the grand old cathedral which Edward the Confessor erected on the site of a still older church more than eight centuries ago. Every English king from Edward the Confessor to Edward the Seventh has been crowned within its walls, with the single exception of Edward the Fifth, who died uncrowned. Every English king or queen from Edward the Confessor down to the time of George the Third has been buried in it, and it has become the last resting-place of those British statesmen, warriors, poets, artists, and men of letters whose names stand high on the roll of fame.

2. To pay a visit to Westminster Abbey is to pass in review the whole history of the British people. A great writer has said: " It seems as if the awful nature of the place presses down upon the soul, and hushes the beholder into noiseless reverence. We feel that we are surrounded by the congregated bones of the great men of past times who have filled the earth with their renown."

3. Let us pay a visit to the Abbey. We make our way to the Chapel of Edward the Confessor, which is behind the high altar. Here we find ourselves in the " burial-place of kings." You will remember seeing a picture of this chapel in Book III. On the north side of the chapel is the tomb of Edward the First, with this inscription in Latin, " *Here lies Edward, Hammer of the Scots. Keep faith.*" When his tomb was opened, in the year 1774, his nickname " Longshanks " was found to be quite appropriate, for the body was six feet two inches in length.

Westminster Abbey.

4. By the side of the stone screen at the other end of the chapel stand two coronation chairs. The one on the left is that which was made for Edward the First. Near

to it you see his sword and shield. Look beneath the seat of the chair. You see a rough piece of sandstone fixed to the chair by iron clamps. It is the ancient stone on which the kings of the Scots sat at their coronation, and is called the *Lia Fail*, or Stone of Destiny. Edward the First brought it from Scone, the ancient capital of Scotland, in 1297, after his great campaign in that country.

5. An old tradition says,—

"If Fates go right, where'er this stone is found
The Scots shall monarchs of that realm be crowned."

The prophecy has been fulfilled, for three hundred and six years after Edward placed the stone in Westminster Abbey a Scottish king was crowned King of England. All British sovereigns since that time have had Scottish blood in their veins.

6. Standing by the side of Edward's tomb, and looking upon the old coronation stone of the Scottish kings, we cannot help thinking of the great attempt which he made to conquer Scotland and unite it with England. Let us very briefly review the history of Scotland up to the time when it fell under the " hammer of the Scots."

7. The history of Caledonia, as Scotland was called in

early times, begins with the invasion of Agricola. After conquering North Wales and what is now Yorkshire, this famous Roman governor of Britain carried his arms into Scotland, which was then a land of vast forests and sterile mountains. He overran the Lowlands, and in order to shut out the natives he built a chain of forts between the Forth and the Clyde.

8. Then he pushed on towards the Highlands, and somewhere in Perthshire defeated the Caledonian chief Galgacus with great slaughter in the year 84 A.D. He was not, however, able to subdue Caledonia, and in later times the Romans abandoned the attempt altogether. As you already know, they built a great stone wall eighty miles long across the moors from Newcastle to Carlisle. Beyond the Clyde and the Forth they did not pretend to rule, and the district between the two walls could scarcely be called Roman, though marked on the map as the province of Valentia.

9. At the close of the sixth century nearly the whole of Scotland to the north of the Firths of Forth and Clyde was in the hands of the Picts. They were divided into Northern Picts and Southern Picts—the latter occupying the country now known as the shires of Perth, Fife, Forfar, and Kincardine. Pictland was divided among a number of tribes, and, as in England, the king of one tribe was sometimes able to get the mastery over two or three others, and make himself the most powerful man in the country.

10. In the south-western part of the country, sometimes called Galloway, sometimes Strathclyde—that is, the valley of the Clyde—Cymric Britons, similar to those of Cornwall

and Wales, held sway. The English conquered the country up to the Firth of Forth, but were only able to settle in the lower lands lying towards the east.

11. The first great event in the history of Scotland is the invasion of a warlike people, who settled down in the land and gave their name to it. While the English were conquering Britain, bands of rovers were crossing the North Channel from Ireland, and were settling down in the islands and along the coast of what is now Argyll-shire. These newcomers are known as the Scots. They set up a kingdom in the west, which gradually became the chief power in the country.

12. The second great event in the history of Scotland is the coming of Columba, an Irish monk, who, in the year 563 A.D., with twelve companions, crossed over from Ireland, and landing on the lonely little island of Iona, near the large island of Mull, built a little wooden church and a number of wattle huts. From this retreat Columba and his friends made missionary journeys to and fro, until they had converted the western part of Scotland. You learnt in Book III. that Aidan, one of Columba's followers, settled at Lindisfarne, or Holy Island, off the Northumbrian coast, and in much the same way taught the Christian faith to the people of Northern England.

13. The kingdom which the Scots set up was not at first called Scotland, but Dalriada. About the year 600 Scotland was divided into four parts. Three of them— Strathclyde, Dalriada, and Pictland—were Celtic; the fourth, which soon afterwards got the name of Lothian, was English.

14. Lothian, which consisted of the south-eastern part of the country, formed the northern division of the kingdom of Northumbria. Edwin, one of Northumbria's most famous kings, built a stronghold on a great volcanic rock near the Forth, and called it Edinburgh—which perhaps means Edwin's castle. From this point the Northumbrians con-quered the low country towards the Clyde, and spread northward along the coast through Fife, and even beyond the Tay. About the year 670 the south-east of Scotland may be said to have been conquered by the English.

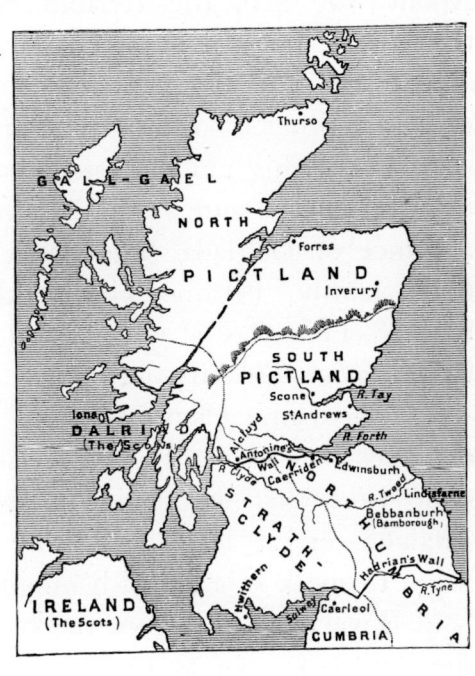

15. In 685 Egfrith, King of Northumbria, led a great army beyond the Forth, with the object of dealing a final blow to the Picts. At Nectan's Mere, in For-farshire, the Pictish king, Brude, defeated and slew him with the greater part of his army. This is one of the most important battles in Scottish history. Had Egfrith won, there would probably have been no kingdom of Scot-land at all. As it was, the Picts and Scots, and the other Celts of Cumbria and Strathclyde, became independent once more.

31. THE STORY OF SCOTLAND.—I.

1. From this time onward for many years the history of Scotland is very difficult to follow. We hear of wars between the Scots in Dalriada and the Celts of Strathclyde, and between the Picts and the Northumbrians. About 800 A.D. the terrible Norsemen began to harry the northern and eastern coasts. This new danger probably forced the Scots, the Picts, and the Celts to unite under one king for the purpose of resisting the invader.

2. How this union came about we do not know; all that we can be sure of is that in 843 Kenneth MacAlpin, a prince of Dalriada, but connected also with the Pictish royal family, became king both of the Picts and the Scots. This was a great event, almost as important as Egbert's overlordship of England.

3. The name Pict soon died out, and the name Scot extended to all the people of Caledonia. Thus about the same time that we begin to speak about a kingdom of England, or, at least, of a king of the English, we can begin to speak of a Scottish kingdom too.

4. Twelve years before the battle of Hastings, Malcolm the Third, known as Canmore or Bighead, became King of Scotland. Much of his life had been spent at the court of Edward the Confessor. His father, King Duncan, had been slain, and he had been driven out of the country by a powerful noble named Macbeth, who had usurped the throne.

5. At length, in 1054, Edward gave Malcolm an army, with which he marched north and overcame Macbeth.

He was crowned at Scone in 1057, and soon after married Margaret, sister of Edgar Atheling, who was the real heir to the English throne, though he had been set aside in favour of Harold.

6. The people of Scotland at that time were much less civilized than their southern neighbours. The marriage of Malcolm with Margaret brought a pious, learned, and gentle lady into the northern land, and she did her utmost to refine the people and improve their condition. Malcolm himself was rough, rude, and half-savage, but the love which he had for his wife taught him to reverence whatever she loved. We are told that he would kiss the sacred books because the queen loved them, and have them bound in the finest bindings for her sake, even though he could not read a word of them. In a hundred different ways Margaret helped to tame this savage king and civilize his court.

7. Malcolm's reign was full of battle and tumult. Five times he crossed the Border with fire and sword, and twice an English king invaded Scotland. Though he struggled hard to maintain the independence of his country, he was forced to acknowledge both William the Conqueror and William Rufus as overlords of Scotland. In the year 1093 Rufus insulted the Scottish king, who determined to wipe out the insult in blood. Hastening to Scotland, he mustered an army and made a raid into England. By treachery he and his eldest son were cut off from the main body and slain. Malcolm's death was a great blow to Scotland.

8. Three sons of Malcolm Canmore became king one after the other. The first of them was Edgar, a gentle, pious king, who reigned during ten years of unbroken

peace. His brother, Alexander the Fierce, who followed him, had something of the spirit of his warlike father. He was also a great friend to the Church, and in his reign numerous monasteries were founded and enriched with lands and money.

9. In 1124 Alexander died without children, and then David, the youngest son of Malcolm Canmore, became king. He was one of the most renowned of Scottish kings, and in his day Scotland stood very high in the roll of nations. She enjoyed peace and prosperity. She was a refuge for exiles and a mart for foreign countries.

10. Henry the First of England was David's brother-in-law, and during the life of the English king there was friendship between the two countries. Henry's declining years, however, were filled with anxiety, because he had only a daughter, Matilda, to succeed him. As you already know, he made the barons, including his nephew Stephen, swear to have Matilda as their queen upon his death. When that event occurred, however, Stephen broke his oath and seized the crown.

11. King David thereupon marched into England to strike a blow for the rights of his niece. Twice he ravaged Northumberland, and treated the inhabitants with great cruelty. In the year 1138 he invaded Yorkshire, but was overcome at the battle of the Standard, near Northallerton.

12. The hero of the battle was the aged Archbishop of York, who assembled the barons and preached a holy war against the Scots. He brought together the banners of the three Yorkshire saints, and set them up on a cart which was wheeled into the fray. On the cart stood the arch-

bishop, praying and cheering his soldiers on to the fight. Again and again the English beat off the wild charges of the Highlanders and Galloway men who formed the bulk of David's army. After two hours' fighting the Scots fled, leaving ten thousand men dead on the field.

13. During the remainder of his life David was busy making changes which completely transformed his kingdom. He founded four bishoprics, introduced monks and friars, and built many of the noble abbeys which are now in ruins, amongst them the famous Abbey of Holyrood at Edinburgh.

14. He overhauled the laws of the kingdom, and on certain days sat at the gate of his palace to do justice to the poor. He encouraged manufactures and trades ; and under him the feudal system, somewhat as described in Lesson 20, was firmly founded in Scotland. The towns also grew to be important and prosperous. Berwick, Roxburgh, Edinburgh, and Stirling united into an association, which continues unto this day.

32. THE STORY OF SCOTLAND.—II.

1. David died in 1153, and was succeeded by his grandson, Malcolm the Maiden, so called because of his girlish appearance. He was a boy of twelve when he was crowned, and was but twenty-four years old when he died and made way for his brother William. This William is known in history as "The Lion," because he took as the royal arms the Scottish Lion, which is still used on the national standard. William had the longest reign of all the Scottish

sovereigns; he ruled from 1165 to 1214, a period of forty-nine years.

2. For a time William the Lion kept on good terms with Henry the Second, but in 1173 he joined a conspiracy against the English king, headed by the son of Henry himself. As the price of his help, young Henry promised William that all the district to the north of the Tyne should be added to the Scottish crown. In the next year William led an army into Northumberland, where the Galloway men repeated their old work of pillage and butchery.

3. One foggy day, while William and his knights were tilting under the walls of Alnwick Castle, a band of English knights approached. William mistook them at first for his own men, but when he discovered his mistake, he cried, " Now we shall see which of us are good knights," and charged into the midst of the foe. He was soon overpowered and made prisoner.

4. Great was the joy of Henry when he heard that the King of Scotland was in his power. He imprisoned the " Lion " in the Castle of Falaise in Normandy. Half a year later William bought his freedom at a heavy price. He was forced to acknowledge himself a vassal of England for the whole of his kingdom, north as well as south of the Forth. Thus the freedom of Scotland was bartered away for the liberty of the king. During the rest of Henry's reign the position of William was by no means pleasant. His subjects were rebellious, but he dared not punish them without Henry's permission.

5. In the reign of Richard the First, however, Scotland bought back her independence, after being a vassal of the

English crown for fifteen years. In 1189, Richard, as you already know, sold his rights over Scotland for a sum of ten thousand marks, which went towards equipping an army for the Crusades. Scotland was once more free.

6. William died in his seventy-fourth year, and during the next seventy-two years Scotland enjoyed her " golden age." At the end of that time, during the reign of the English king, Edward the First, Alexander the Third, while riding in the dusk towards Kinghorn, on the coast of Fifeshire, fell over the cliff and was killed. His death was a great blow to Scotland, and never was a Scottish sovereign so much lamented. His daughter Margaret, who had been married to Eric of Norway, had died three years before. Her infant daughter, also named Margaret, and known as the Maid of Norway, was now the heiress to the crown of Scotland.

7. A meeting of the nobles and clergy was held at Scone, and six guardians were elected to govern the kingdom. Then the " Estates," as the Parliament of Scotland was called, proposed that Edward's eldest son should marry the Maid of Norway, and thus, on the English king's death, the crowns would be united, and the strife of the two countries ended. Nothing happier could have been arranged. Unfortunately, however, the Maid died during the voyage to Scotland, and at once difficulties arose.

8. A round dozen of claimants to the throne immediately appeared, the two most important of them being John Baliol, great-grandson of David, William the Lion's brother, and Robert Bruce, grandson of the same. Bruce, as the son of David's *second* daughter, was nearer to the

royal stock than Baliol, who was the grandson of David's *eldest* daughter.   Baliol, however, was more directly descended from David.   Edward proposed himself as umpire to decide between the would-be kings, and summoned the Scottish barons and clergy to meet him at Norham Castle in May 1291.

9. Before giving his decision, Edward insisted on being recognized as overlord of Scotland.   The candidates to the throne, anxious to secure the umpire's good-will, consented ; and then Edward gave judgment in favour of John Baliol, who was crowned, and paid homage to Edward as his overlord.

10. Now, Edward meant to be overlord of Scotland in very deed, and in a variety of ways he soon showed Baliol that he regarded him as nothing more than a vassal.   This roused the Scots to bitter anger, and they forced Baliol to ally himself with France, and to send bands of raiders across the Border.

11. Edward marched north with a great host, crossed the Tweed, mercilessly stormed the frontier fortress of Berwick, and three weeks later defeated the Scottish army with great slaughter.   Edinburgh, Stirling, and Perth fell into his hands, and in six months the conquest of Scotland was complete.   Baliol was deposed, and allowed to retire to Normandy, where he died in 1314.   When Edward returned to England he took with him the " Stone of Destiny."

12. Edward thought that he had tamed Scotland, just as he had tamed Wales, but he was mistaken.   In less than a year the people of the West Lowlands were up in arms, under the leadership of a Strathclyde squire, William

Wallace of Ellerslie. The revolt spread all over the Lowlands, and Edward's army, under the command of the Earl of Surrey, was overwhelmed at the battle of Stirling Bridge in 1297. All the fruits of Edward's conquest were destroyed at a blow. The Scottish barons, who had hitherto held aloof, now joined Wallace, who not only recovered all Scotland, but crossed the Tweed and cruelly ravaged the northern shires.

13. In 1298 Edward marched north again. He met Wallace at Falkirk, and completely overcame him. The Scots continued the struggle, but five years later the whole country was subdued. Wallace was captured and executed in 1305 ; but within a year of Wallace's death a third revolt began under Robert Bruce, the grandson of the Bruce who had been a claimant for the crown in 1291. He was one of the two men who now claimed the crown. The other was John Comyn, a son of John Baliol's sister. Bruce stabbed his rival in Dumfries Church, and gathering his followers at Scone, had himself crowned in March 1306.

14. At first his rebellion seemed to be a failure, and his army was dispersed by Edward's general. With a price on his head, Bruce was forced to seek shelter in the Highlands, and Edward treated his followers with great cruelty. These harsh measures brought many recruits to Bruce's standard.

15. The rebellion gained strength, and the stern, white-haired old English king mounted his horse and rode slowly towards Scotland for the third and last time. He died three miles from the Border, and with his latest breath he made his miserable son, Edward the Second, swear to con-

tinue the conquest. The new Edward, however, had no intention of keeping his oath. He turned back, and went home, to fling himself into the arms of worthless favourites.

16. A small force advanced into Scotland, but it could make no headway against the forces of Bruce. One strong place after another fell into his hands, and at last Stirling Castle alone was left. Even the craven Edward was now aroused, and in June 1314 he marched with a large army into Scotland. On the twenty-fourth of the same month a battle was fought at Bannockburn, two miles south of Stirling. It ended, as you already know, in the total defeat of the English. By this great victory Scotland won back her independence.

33. THE WOOLSACK.

1. To-day we will make our way to the Palace of West-minster, which we have already visited, and peep into the House of Lords. It is a magnificent chamber, wonderfully adorned with gilding, statues, stained-glass windows, and wall paintings. The twelve windows contain portraits of the kings and queens of England, and the statues in the niches represent the barons who compelled King John to sign Magna Charta.

2. At the south end, beneath a great gilded canopy, is the throne on which the King takes his seat when he opens or closes Parliament. To the right of the King's throne is another throne for the Queen, and on either side are lower thrones for the Prince and Princess of Wales.

THE WOOLSACK IN THE HOUSE OF LORDS.

3. We have not come to admire the glories of the House of Lords, but to look at the quaint, cushioned seat immediately in front of the throne. It is known as the "Woolsack," and on it sits the Lord Chancellor, who is chairman of the House of Lords. The "Woolsack" is nothing but a large square bag covered with red cloth and stuffed with wool, yet it stands for a great historic fact. It was first placed in the House of Lords by Edward the Third, to indicate that wool was the chief source of England's wealth. Wool has long ceased to be our most important product, and coal has now taken its place. Were

the present King to imitate the example of Edward the Third, the Lord Chancellor would sit upon a coalsack !

4. In the days of Edward the First wool was the staple trade of England. At this time nearly all the people were engaged in farming. Let me try to give you a picture of the way in which farming was then carried on. Many of the great lords owned estates in various parts of England, and each separate estate or manor was managed by a bailiff. One-third of the arable land of a manor was called the demesne or domain, and was kept for the lord's own use ; the remaining two-thirds were parcelled out amongst the villagers, some having as much as thirty acres, others little more than a garden.

5. Some of these villagers were freemen, who paid rent in money, but most of them were serfs or villeins, who paid rent in labour or in kind. They had to plough and reap and do other work on the demesne for two or three days every week throughout the year, and to give whatever extra time was needed at harvest and on other occasions. Besides this, many of them had to give their lord a small tribute of eggs or fowls or wheat at certain times in the year, in return for which he provided them with meals of herrings, bread, and beer when they were working for him.

6. The whole estate, both the lord's demesne and the portion divided amongst the villagers, was cultivated as one farm ; and this was necessary, because each man's land was not separated from the rest, but consisted of acre or half-acre strips scattered about in various parts of the estate.

7. The ploughing was done with great wooden ploughs drawn by oxen, and, as you may imagine, the ground was

not very well turned up.   On the best lands in good years each acre produced about sixteen bushels of wheat—that is, about a third of what is now produced on the same soil.   During the winter the wheat was threshed and winnowed, and carefully stored in barns or granges, and sometimes in churches.   Rarely was more produced than sufficient to support the lord and the villagers until the next harvest.

8. The live stock consisted of sheep, cattle, a few horses, and many pigs.   In the summer all these animals were sent out together under the care of cowherds, shepherds, and swineherds, to feed on the pastures and in the woods and wastes which surrounded the estate.   When winter drew near most of the cattle were killed and their flesh salted for food.

9. By far the most important of the live stock were the sheep, for sheep-farming was the most profitable occupation of the time.   The sheep were small and their fleeces very light.   About one in five perished every year from rot and scab and the hardships of the winter.   Nevertheless, wool was " the sovereign treasure of the kingdom."

10. England was very favourably situated for sheep-farming.   Her climate and soil were suitable, and unlike the countries of the Continent she was a peaceful land, where these tender and defenceless animals could feed in security.   Flanders, which was the great woollen manufacturing country, was only a short voyage away, and every week during the summer swarms of light craft crossed the North Sea laden with English wool.   Nine-tenths of the wool went to Bruges and Ghent, where the townsfolk

depended upon it to supply their looms, just as the mill hands of Lancashire nowadays depend upon the cotton which comes from America.

11. Edward the First was the first king to regulate the wool trade, and to make it provide him with the sinews of war and peace. When he began the conquest of Wales, he levied a tax of six shillings and eightpence on every sack of wool exported from the country, and with the money so obtained he paid his men-at-arms. No subject was allowed to export wool on pain of loss of life or limb. The business was in the hands of a body of merchants licensed by the king, and all the wool exported had to be weighed and certified by the king's officers, who also collected the tax.

12. Ten towns, called "staple towns," were set apart for the sale of wool, and it could be sold nowhere else. Each of these towns had its own port, from which the wool was shipped abroad. Now I think you begin to understand how important the wool trade was, and how suitable it was that the highest officer of the State should take his seat on a woolsack.

13. Before I close this lesson, let me tell you about a great change which was taking place at this time in the condition of the villeins on the manors up and down the country. In earlier times the serfs were bound to the soil. They belonged to the lord of the manor, and were just as much his property as his horses and oxen. They were not allowed to leave their manor and go elsewhere to seek work without their lord's permission. In the time of Edward the First the villeins were rapidly changing from serfs into servants.

14. This change was brought about, not by the goodwill of the lords, but because they could not get their land properly tilled by the forced labour of the serfs. The villagers naturally worked hard on their own land, but did as little as possible on their lord's land, and thus the demesnes could not be farmed at a profit.

15. At this time, too, the lords began to need ready money to keep up the pomp and state which became the fashion of the time. They therefore allowed their villeins to pay money-rents instead of labour-rents, and this practice gradually grew. Thus, in order to find the labour necessary to cultivate their demesnes, they had to hire the villeins to do the work, and these men thus became paid labourers.

16. When the lord had sufficient labourers to work his demesne, he cared little whether the rest of the labourers stayed on his manor or not. Often he was willing to let them seek employment elsewhere on payment of a small fine. Thus we find large numbers of villeins gradually becoming free tenants. We shall learn in a later lesson how serfdom entirely passed away.

---

34. THE LONG=BOW.

1. To-day we will visit the churchyard of an old English village. We are not going to look at the church, with its time-worn tower and its mantle of ivy; nor are we going to read the epitaphs on the ancient tombstones, beneath which the "rude forefathers of the hamlet sleep." We are going to see a group of noble yew trees. They are

The Maid.

(*From the picture by Frank Craig in the Royal Academy of 1907.   By special permission of the Artist.*)

tall evergreen trees, with thick trunks and great branches. Their wood is hard, springy, smooth, and tough. We shall find yew trees in many of the old churchyards of England.

2. If you are thoughtful, you will perhaps ask yourself why yew trees should have been planted in so many of our churchyards. Well, first of all, they are solemn and gloomy looking trees, and seem suitable for the place where the dead lie buried. There is another reason too. Before the days of gunpowder our forefathers used bows in their warfare. The wood of the yew makes the best of bows. Yew trees were planted in the churchyards because their wood in olden days supplied the men of the village with their bows.

3. Here is a verse of a stirring song, called " The Bow-men of England " :—

> " What of the bow ?
> The bow was made in England,
> Of yew wood, of true wood,
> The wood of English bows.
> So men who are free
> Love the old yew tree,
> And the land where the yew tree grows."

4. The long-bowmen of England never had their peers. They were the flower of the archers of the world. We are not quite sure which nation first used the long-bow, but we do know that in the year 1252, during the reign of Henry the Third, all men with more than forty shillings and less than one hundred shillings in land, and all towns-men with goods worth more than nine and less than twenty marks, were ordered to take the field with bow and arrows, instead of the lance as formerly.

5. Up to that time the heavily-armed horseman was the chief power in battle. His day, however, was fast passing away. Simon de Montfort was the last English general to win victories by the charges of heavy cavalry alone. In the days of Edward the First, his great pupil, the long-bow became the national weapon. With the six-foot bow and the clothyard shaft Edward's archers triumphed over the Welsh and the Scots.

6. The battle of Falkirk was won almost entirely by the bow, and one of the reasons why Bannockburn was lost in the reign of Edward the Second was because that miserable son of a great father did not know how to use archers. "He put them," says a writer of the time, "behind the knights, instead of on their flanks, and bade them fire over their heads ; hence they hit some few Scots in the breast, but struck many more of their own friends in the back."

7. So important did Edward the First and his successors consider the art of archery that a law was made ordering every man, except judges and clergymen, to possess a bow of his own height, and keep it ready for use. A father had also to give bows to his sons, and see that from ten years of age and upwards they were trained to shoot. Butts were set up in every parish, and the men had to practise at them on one day in each week. If they did not do so they were fined.

8. Englishmen were nearly all brought up to the use of the bow, and their marksmanship was extraordinary. Their bows could carry a clothyard shaft three hundred yards with such force that it would pierce everything that was not protected by armour. At a shorter range it would

even pierce the steel plates with which knights then covered their bodies. Robin Hood, you will remember, was the prince of bowmen. According to an old tale, he once shot an arrow two miles and an inch! I am afraid that the man who told the story was "drawing the long-bow" in quite another way.

9. Under Edward the Third the English bowmen did their most notable deeds. You already know that Edward the Third tried to win the crown of France for himself. He began a war with the French which lasted on and off for one hundred years. I shall tell you about this war in the next lesson. In the seventh year of the war the famous battle of Crécy was fought, and was won almost entirely by the archers. Let me describe this battle.

10. The English line was in two divisions. In each of the divisions there were about two thousand archers and eight hundred men-at-arms. The archers in each division were drawn up on the slope of a gentle hill, and were arranged like the points of a harrow, so that each man in the second line could shoot between two of the first. King Philip had an army five or six times as strong as that of the English, and it consisted almost wholly of horse-soldiers in armour. In front of his line of mailed knights were Genoese cross-bowmen.

11. The cross-bowmen began the battle, but they were almost useless against the English archers. Their bow-strings had been wetted and made slack by the rain, while those of the English had been kept dry. At its best the cross-bow was a clumsy weapon. While the Genoese was . winding up his bow for a single shot, the English archer

could fire half-a-dozen arrows. The long-bow had also a longer range, so that the cross-bowmen were shot down and dispersed before they were able to do much mischief.

12. Then the knights advanced, riding through or over the routed cross-bowmen. At once the English archers began to fire long, steady volleys at the advancing line. Down went men and horses "in one red burial blent." Soon a great heap of wounded and dead lay before the archers, and this ghastly barrier prevented the knights from riding them down. Only here and there did the Frenchmen come to hand strokes with the English men-at-arms.

13. For some hours the battle surged along the English front, while the arrows whistled through the air with deadly effect. At nightfall the French knights fled, leaving a quarter of their whole army dead or dying on the stricken field. Thus the battle was won, and the archers had not moved a single pace from their first position. Nine years later, at Poictiers, our bowmen gained another great victory.

14. Edward's great-grandson, Henry the Fifth, continued the war, and once again the English archers won great renown. At Agincourt the English line of battle was formed in much the same way as at Crécy, only that each of the archers carried an ironshod stake, which he planted in the ground before him as a protection against the charge of cavalry. The ground in front was a slippery ploughed field, and in this the knights, weighed down by their heavy armour, were almost powerless.

15. Well-nigh every horse and most of the riders were shot down before they reached the archers at all. Some of them stuck fast in the mire, and when Henry gave the

order for his whole army to charge, the lightly-clad archers slung their bows on their backs, and with axe, mace, and sword fell upon the hampered knights, and soon settled the day. The French lost ten thousand men at Agincourt, the English scarcely a hundred.

16. The bow continued to be the national weapon right down to the reign of Elizabeth, at which time the heavy gun and the musket, known as the arquebus, were in general use both at home and abroad. The fleet which scattered the Armada contained many archers. Not until the seventeenth century did the long-bow finally give place to firearms.

35. THE HUNDRED YEARS' WAR.—I.

1. You remember that when we visited Westminster Abbey and saw the Coronation Stone, I pointed out to you the shield of Edward the Third, which stood close by.

SHIELD OF EDWARD III.   SHIELD OF PHILIP VI.

Here is a picture of it. You notice that it is divided into four parts or quarters. In the second and third quarters are three lions *passant gardant*—that is, walking and looking out from the shield. These stand for England.

2. In the first and fourth quarters are figures which are supposed to resemble lilies. Here is a picture of the royal shield of Philip the Sixth, who was King of France when Edward the Third was King of England. You notice that it is strewn with these lilies, the *fleurs de lys* as they are called.

3. Now you see that Edward the Third has quartered the royal arms of France on his shield side by side with the royal arms of England. What does this mean? It means that Edward the Third, the grandson of the " hammer of the Scots," claims to be King of France as well as King of England. This claim was persisted in by several later sovereigns, and the lilies of France appeared upon the shields of English kings and queens down to the beginning of the 19th century.

4. Our connection with France has been very long and very close. Edward the Confessor, you will remember, had lived for many years in Normandy before he succeeded to the English crown. He brought over hosts of French friends, and these paved the way for the coming of a French king. When William, Duke of Normandy, conquered England, Frenchmen became masters of this country. I told you in Lesson 20 what an important influence the Norman-French language, ideas, and manners had upon the English people.

5. When the Duke of Normandy became King of England the sorrows of England began. They did not end until English dominion in France was entirely lost. Many of William's Norman barons possessed estates both in Normandy and in England. They regarded Normandy

as their mother country, and England as a conquered land from which they drew tribute. They despised the English, and refused to throw in their lot with them.

6. When, however, the French possessions of the English kings were lost, the barons had to choose whether they would be Frenchmen or Englishmen. Those great families which had estates on both sides of the English Channel divided into two branches. One branch became French, and, in the course of time, the other branch became English.

7. Henry the Second, you will remember, was master of the greater part of France. He wore the gilt coronet of Normandy in succession to his mother, and by his marriage with Eleanor he obtained such a large and rich territory in the south of France that he actually held sway over more French country than the King of France himself. In the reign of the wicked King John most of these possessions were lost, except the rich and fertile province of Gascony.

8. The French kings cast longing eyes on the fair lands which still remained in the hands of the English, and constantly strove to win them back. They kept nibbling at the frontier, and by the time Edward the Third came to the throne they had seized a number of towns, which they refused to give up. This was the chief cause of the long struggle known in history as the Hundred Years' War.

9. Another important reason for the war was that the French king was trying hard to crush the people of Flanders, which, as you know, was the country which made cloth out of English wool. Edward knew that the prosperity of

his kingdom depended upon the friendship of the great cloth-working towns of Flanders. If these towns fell into the hands of France, England's great wool trade would be in danger. Edward soon saw that war could not be avoided, and, in the year 1337, for the second time, he boldly put forth a claim to the French throne.

10. On the death of Charles the Fourth, nine years before, Edward had been one of the three claimants to the French throne. He had claimed through his mother Isabella, the daughter of Philip the Fourth of France. Philip's three sons had reigned, and had died leaving only daughters to succeed them. The real heir to the throne was Charles, the grandson of Philip's eldest son, and he, like Edward, claimed through his mother.

11. The French lawyers held that the law of France forbade a woman to wear the crown. Edward replied that though his mother had no claim, she could pass one on to her son. The French lawyers had laughed at the idea, and had set both the claimants aside in favour of Philip of Valois, a cousin of the late king. When Edward decided on war, Philip had been reigning for ten years.

12. In the long war that was now to begin England had three great advantages over France—she had a better fleet, and thus soon won the command of the sea ; her archers were far better shots than those of France ; and her generals were more skilful. On land Edward was unsuccessful at first, but at sea he was able to destroy the whole French fleet, and thus free England from the danger of invasion. The English people were delighted at this victory, and forthwith dubbed Edward "King of the Sea."

Edward the Third at the Siege of Calais.

(From the painting by Sir John Gilbert, R.A. By permission of the Corporation of London.)

36. THE HUNDRED YEARS' WAR.—II.

1. In the seventh year of the war Edward landed at La Hogue in Normandy, and on August 26, 1346, he fought the great battle of Crécy, which you read about in Lesson 34. Then he pushed on to besiege Calais, which was little better than a nest of pirates who continually preyed on English shipping. Calais stands in a flat and marshy country, and in those days only three roads crossed the marsh to the city. Edward held these roads, and also blockaded Calais by sea.

2. Outside the walls he built a wooden town, which he called "Newtown the Bold," and there he sat for eight months. Meanwhile the Scots, who were the allies of the French, invaded England, but were badly beaten at Nevil's Cross, and their king, David Bruce, was taken prisoner. He was kept in captivity for eleven long years, and was only allowed to return to Scotland after promising to pay a ransom which in our days would amount to about a million and a quarter sterling.

3. Calais suffered terribly, and Philip tried to relieve it, but in vain, and in the year 1347 the city surrendered. It was of the highest value to the English kings so long as the Hundred Years' War lasted, for it provided them with an open doorway into France. You may be sure that the French felt the loss keenly.

4. The war began again in 1355, and at Poictiers the Black Prince, Edward's eldest son, utterly overthrew a great French army which was trying to cut him off from the town of Bordeaux. In the fight King John, the successor

of Philip, was captured, and, as you already know, was treated in a most knightly manner by the Black Prince. Despite the king's capture, the war continued for four years, and then peace was made.

5. Look at a map of France, and find the river Loire. You will notice that one of its left-bank tributaries is called the Vienne. Almost all the country between the Loire and the Vienne on the north, and the Pyrenees on the south, was the English king's land after peace was made. Strange to say, however, these great conquests were soon lost. During the last seven years of Edward's reign, one place after another fell into the hands of the French. Before Edward lay in his grave, his dominions in France had dwindled down to the ports of Bordeaux and Bayonne and the fortress of Calais.

6. The French were not satisfied to rest and be thankful while the English held any part of France at all. They therefore continued the war off and on during the unhappy reign of Richard the Second, the eldest son of the Black Prince, who had died during the lifetime of his father. In Richard's reign troubles abounded in England, and some of them we shall read of in a later lesson. At last the country was in such a state of confusion that Parliament made the king give up his throne to his cousin Henry the Fourth, the son of Edward the Third's third son.

7. Henry, like his grandfather, Edward the Third, and his uncle, the Black Prince, would gladly have sought fortune and fame in a war with France. He had, however, no opportunity of doing so, for plots and rebellions at home kept him busy and anxious for more than half his reign.

When at last the land was at peace, he was too old and feeble to have heart for such an undertaking.

8. His son, Henry the Fifth, was in a very different position. He was young and handsome, a fine soldier, and very popular with his subjects. He soon saw that nothing would make England peaceful at home but war abroad. He therefore renewed the war with France, and in this enterprise he had the whole of England at his back. France at the time was ruled by a mad king, and was much weakened by the quarrels of her princes and nobles.

9. Henry set up the old claim of Edward the Third, and demanded all the old French possessions of the English kings. Of course his demand was refused. Parliament gave him liberal grants of money, and the king even pawned the crown jewels to get the means wherewith to equip his archers and men-at-arms. He set sail late in the summer of 1415, and landed at Harfleur. Seven weeks were occupied in capturing the town ; and by the end of the siege his army was so much reduced that he resolved to march along the coast to Calais, and there await the coming of fresh troops from England.

10. The English were weary and footsore, wasted by disease, and weakened by want of food. They crossed the Somme, only to find an army of Frenchmen, five times as great as their own, blocking the way to Calais. Next day, October 25, 1415, the famous battle of Agincourt took place. You already know that the French were hopelessly beaten. The English actually slew a greater number of men than there were in the whole of their own ranks.

11. A great welcome awaited Henry and his army in

England, and preparations were at once made for a further invasion of France. Two years later he crossed the Channel again, and by 1419 he was master of the whole of Normandy. The French nobles, by their bitter quarrels, played into Henry's hands ; and in the next year the French king, Charles the Sixth, was forced to make a treaty, by which Henry was to marry his daughter, the Princess Catherine, to be regent of France, and his successor on the throne. The Dauphin, the French king's eldest son, refused to be bound by any such treaty, and continued the war.

12. Henry was master of France for little more than two years. In 1422 he died at the early age of thirty-five, worn out by the fatigues of many campaigns. His son Henry was a baby less than a year old. The baby-king's uncle, John of Bedford, became regent, and he carried on the war with France. He was an able soldier and a wise man. For a time he held his own, and even won several victories ; then the tide of fortune began to turn.

13. In 1429 the first great blow was dealt at the English power. The English soldiers had laid siege to Orleans, and were on the point of taking it, when Joan of Arc, clad in knightly armour and displaying a white banner before her, rode at the head of the Dauphin's army to the relief of the city. This famous girl was a peasant from Lorraine. She believed that she had been chosen by Heaven to save France from the English.

14. Joan entered the city, and led the garrison in their assaults on the besiegers. The first attack was successful, and then the people of Orleans hailed her as a deliverer sent by God. The English dreaded her approach, and were

forced to raise the siege. Everywhere they were driven back, and three months later the Dauphin was crowned as Charles the Seventh at Rheims. In the spring of the next year Joan was sold to the English, and in 1431 was burned as a witch in the market-place of Rouen ; but even this cruel act did not stem the tide of French success. Bedford died in 1435, and the English power in France slowly but surely passed away. By 1453 nothing was left of all the English conquests but the town of Calais.

37. CHAUCER'S PILGRIMS.—I.

1. Come with me to the ancient city of Canterbury. It stands amidst the gentle hills of Kent, on the banks of the little river Stour. There is no city in all England that can teach us more history than Canterbury. The Romans had a station on the spot where the city now stands, and the English who first settled in the place were the Jutes who came over with Hengist and Horsa.

2. Parts of the old walls remain, and the battered keep of a Norman castle may still be seen. There are many ancient churches in the city, and one of them is the oldest in all the land. It is called St. Martin's Church, and is partly built of Roman brick. It is said that this church was erected for Queen Bertha, the wife of King Ethelbert, who was baptized by Augustine more than thirteen hundred years ago.

3. The glory of Canterbury, however, is its magnificent cathedral. Ever since the days of Augustine there has been a great church on this spot. A fire swept the first cathedral away a year after the battle of Hastings. A still grander

building arose on its ruins, but this too was destroyed by fire in the reign of Henry the Second. Then the most skilful builders and workmen in England and France were brought to the city, and slowly the present cathedral arose. All down the centuries, arches and windows, chapels and towers, have been added to it, and now it is one of the most splendid temples in all the world.

4. We might easily spend the whole day in gazing at the ancient tombs, statues, and painted windows, but time presses. We may not even pause by the tomb of the Black Prince, and examine his helmet, coat of mail, and shield, which hang above it. We must push on to the northern arm of the cross-shaped building. We are now standing near the spot where an Archbishop of Canterbury was murdered in his own cathedral. You know that his name was Becket, and that he lived in the days of Henry the Second, the great law reformer, who first sent the judges on their circuits and established what has grown into trial by jury.

5. Becket, as you read in Book III., stood up against the king for the rights of the priests. You will remember that in his day the clergy were outside the ordinary law altogether. They enjoyed what was called "benefit of clergy," and this privilege enabled many criminals who were not really clergymen to go unpunished.

6. King and archbishop quarrelled on this and other matters, and the quarrel grew more and more bitter, until one day the king in a fit of rage asked if no one would rid him of "this proud priest." Some of his knights took him at his word, and two days before the end of the year

1170 they killed him near to the spot on which we are now standing.

7. After Becket's death he was made a saint. A shrine of wonderful beauty was set up, and it blazed with jewels and cloth of gold. It stood on yonder pavement to the east of the high altar. When the shrine was taken down its treasures filled twenty-six carts. The steps leading up to it were deeply worn by the knees of the countless men and women who for three hundred years came from far and near to pray at the shrine of St. Thomas of Canterbury.

8. Now, one of our great English poets, named Geoffrey Chaucer, has left us a wonderful picture of the kind of men and women who came as pilgrims to Canterbury. Chaucer tells us that in his time—that is, more than two hundred years after the murder of Becket—people considered a visit to the tomb of St. Thomas the occasion for a merry picnic.

9. Chaucer tells us how a party of thirty-four met at the Tabard Inn in Southwark, and, mounting on their nags, rode along the pleasant Kentish lanes towards the shrine of St. Thomas, under the guidance of " mine host," who kept the company in order and made all the arrangements for the journey. The pilgrims were obliged to travel in a party, because highway robbers lurked about the roads, waiting to attack solitary wayfarers.

10. Now let us look at Chaucer's pilgrims as they amble along, and we shall get an excellent idea of our forefathers in the reigns of Edward the Third and Richard the Second. First comes a knight mounted on a fine charger. He has just come back from the wars, and his jerkin is stained with the rust of the armour which he has but lately taken off.

He has fought on fifteen deadly battlefields, but he is as meek and gentle as a maid. He is, in sooth, "a very perfect, gentle knight."

11. His son, a curly-headed squire, rides by his father's side. He is dressed in a gay gown of bright colours, according to the latest fashion of the court, and he is the very life and soul of the party. He can ride, tilt, dance, sing, play on the flute, make verses, and draw pictures. He is a very gallant youth indeed.

38. CHAUCER'S PILGRIMS.—II.

1. The knight and squire have one servant with them—a brown-faced gamekeeper, with a hood and coat of green. Under his belt is a sheaf of arrows, in his hand is a bow, and by his side are a sword and buckler. He is a master of woodcraft, and loves to tell stories of Robin Hood.

2. Yonder is a prioress—that is, a lady at the head of a house in which nuns live. She is beautiful, her dress is well made, and she wears a pretty bracelet of coral and gold. She is "full simple and coy," very refined, amiable, and tender-hearted, and her manners at table are perfect. She never lets anything drop on her breast, and she does not dip her fingers *too far* into the sauce. With her are a nun and three priests.

3. Not far away are a fat monk, a lazy friar, and a crafty pardoner. We shall hear more of these characters in the next lesson. Chaucer has many a sly home-thrust at these churchmen, but he has nothing but praise for the poor

country parson, a simple, patient, godly man, who lives a good life, and does his duty well.

> " Cristes love and His Apostles' twelve
> He taught, and ferst he folwed it himselve."

With him is his brother, an honest ploughman.

4. Amongst the other pilgrims are a lawyer, a clever man, full of learning and wisdom ; a doctor of physic dressed in a blood-red garment ; a scholar of Oxford, who loves books better than anything else in the world, and spends all his money on them ; a merchant, who is very sharp and hard in his bargains ; a tanned shipman, who has been many voyages ; a cook, a weaver, a dyer, an upholsterer, a haberdasher, a carpenter, a miller, and a reeve ; and a lady of fashion, with a round, red face, a hat as big as a shield, a kerchief of fine cloth, stockings of scarlet, and new shoes. Another of the company is an old franklin or yeoman, who is fond of good living, and is famed for his hospitality.

5. Finally comes Chaucer himself, the " father of English poetry " and " the well of English undefiled," as he has been called.   He was the son of a London wine merchant, and was born about the year 1340.   In his seventeenth year he became page to the wife of Edward the Third's third son, John of Gaunt, Duke of Lancaster. Two years later we find him serving under Edward the Third in the French campaign, where he was taken prisoner. On his release he became one of the valets of the king's chamber, and several times he was sent abroad to Flanders, France, and Italy on the king's service.

6. In 1374 he was given an important post in con-

nection with the customs, and was granted a pension by John of Gaunt, to whose party he attached himself. In 1386 he became one of the knights of the shire for Kent, and sat in Parliament. In later years he was deprived of his offices, and was reduced to something like poverty. Towards the close of his life, however, fortune again smiled on him, for Henry the Fourth, the son of his old protector, John of Gaunt, gave him a new pension in addition to his old one. He died in the year 1400, and his tomb is in Poets' Corner, Westminster Abbey, beneath a stained-glass window representing scenes from "The Canterbury Tales."

7. Chaucer is one of the greatest of our English poets. His verses are very melodious, and as we read them we feel that we are in the company of a large-minded, happy, gentle, observant, and quietly humorous man, with a great love for birds and flowers, trees and sunshine. Chaucer wrote numerous other works besides "The Canterbury Tales"—that is, the series of stories which the pilgrims told to one another to while away the long hours of their journey. His great service to our tongue, however, was in helping to establish a written language common to all England.

8. At the time when Chaucer was born, English was a despised tongue ; the language of the court and of educated men was Norman-French. Gradually, however, a great change took place. Norman baron and Englishman drew closer together, and began to respect each other more and more. In the wars with France the English archers won glorious victories over the French, and the language of the beaten foe lost caste in England. In 1362 Edward

the Third caused a law to be passed which ordered the English language to be used henceforth in the law courts. Thus English became once more the official language of England.

9. At this time, however, there were several dialects of English spoken in the country. Chaucer wrote in the dialect of the south-east Midlands—that is, of London—and this, in course of time, became the literary language of England. The new English, however, was not the old English ; it was enriched with numerous words taken from the French, and thus became, in the fourteenth century, an instrument capable of expressing the deepest thoughts of sages and the finest fancies of poets. Chaucer laid the foundations of our literary tongue, and in this lies his greatest claim to our gratitude.

39. THE LOLLARDS.

1. In Chaucer's day the Church had fallen away from its old simple, pious ways. Many of the monks lived idle and careless lives, and the friars, who had done such splendid work amongst the poor and the outcast, had lost much of their old zeal, and no longer kept up the strict rule of poverty.

2. Chaucer describes the monk in his band of Canterbury pilgrims as a keen hunting man, who kept greyhounds, and had many a dainty horse in his stable. When he rode, men might hear his bridle jingling as loud and clear as the chapel bell. He no longer followed the rule of

his order, nor did he work with his hands or sit poring over a book in the cloister. His robe was edged with costly fur, and he fastened his hood under his chin with an elaborate brooch made of gold. He was portly and jolly, and "a fat swan loved he best of any roast."

3. The friar whom Chaucer describes was equally worldly in his life and tastes. He had a licence from the Pope which permitted him to supersede the priests even in their own parishes. He was "the best beggar in his house," and by gossip and flattery he got great store of alms from the good-wives to whom he sold knives and pins. He could sing a merry song, and he knew and frequented every tavern in the towns through which he passed. His short cloak was of doubled worsted ; and he lisped as he spoke, in order to make his English sound sweet upon the tongue.

4. Another of Chaucer's churchmen was a pardoner, whose wallet was brimful of pardons "come from Rome all hot." Those who bought these pardons were freed from penances on account of their sin. He carried also relics of the saints, and by the sale of these he made more money in one day than a small farmer would make in a year. By his tricks and deceits he made "the people his apes."

5. At this time many serious and thoughtful men wished to do away with the abuses which were bringing the Church into disrepute. Amongst these men was John Wycliffe, an Oxford scholar, who first became prominent towards the end of Edward the Third's reign. He was a learned, grave, and very earnest man, who loved his country, and was greatly opposed to the power of the Pope in England. When the Parliament refused the Pope's claim

to a yearly tribute of a thousand marks, Wycliffe wrote a book, in which he denied that the Pope was the king of earthly kings. He also said that the king and the Parliament were supreme in all matters, whether relating to the Church or anything else.

6. Wycliffe poured contempt on the luxury of the clergy, and on the begging friars, who were the great supporters of the Pope in this country. Then he went on to deny many of the doctrines taught by the Church, and for this reason he is known as "the morning star of the Reformation"—that is, the herald of the great change in the religion of the English people which took place in Tudor times.

7. Come with me to the little Midland town of Lutterworth in South Leicestershire, eighty miles from London. It is a quiet little place, built on the slope of a hill descending to the waters of the river Swift, a tributary of the Avon. There is nothing much to interest us in Lutterworth, except the large stone church with its lofty tower. Inside you will see a portrait of Wycliffe, and you will be shown the pulpit in which he preached and the gown which he wore. He was parish priest of Lutterworth from 1374 to 1384.

8. Wycliffe was a preacher of wonderful power, and he organized bands of men, whom he sent out to speak to the people in churchyards, at fairs, in market-places, and wherever they could be gathered together. His greatest work, however, was to translate the Scriptures from the Latin into English. Parts of the Bible had been translated before, but now for the first time the English people had the whole of the sacred book in their own tongue.

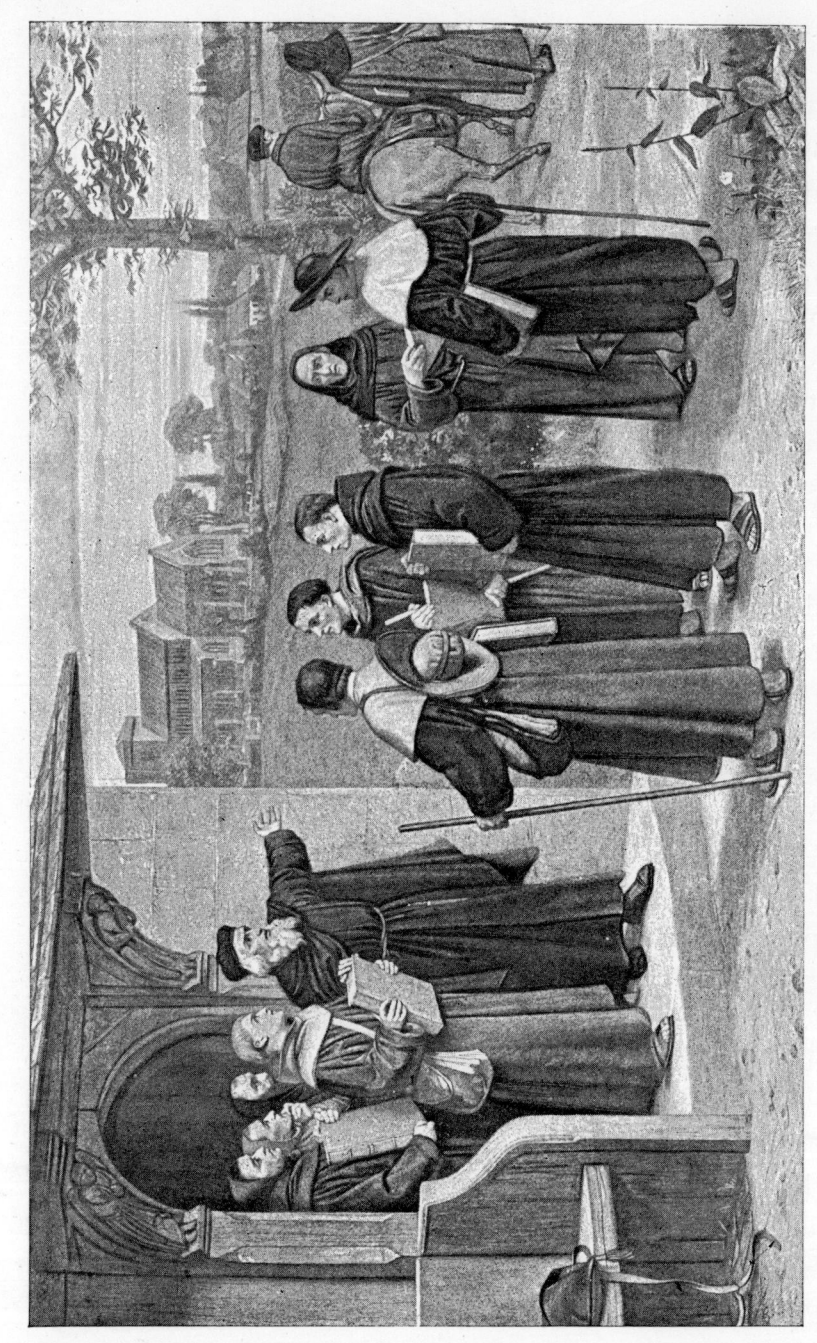

THE DAWN OF THE REFORMATION.

(From the picture by W. F. Yeames, R.A.   By permission of Messrs. Henry Graves and Co.)

9. Printing had not been invented, so copies of the Bible had to be written out slowly with the pen.   A Bible in those days was a most expensive book, but people were so eager to read it that they clubbed together their pennies to buy a copy.   It is said that for a few leaves of the New Testament farmers were ready to give a load of hay.

10. The circulation of Wycliffe's Bible led to a large increase in the number of persons who wished to reform the Church.   Attempts were made to stop Wycliffe's preaching, and to have him thrust out of his living, but in vain. He died at Lutterworth in 1384, and was buried in the graveyard of his church.

11. Some forty-four years after his death his bones were dug up, burnt to ashes, and thrown into the Swift.   An old writer says : " Thus this brook hath conveyed his ashes into Avon ; Avon into Severn ; Severn into the narrow seas ; they into the main ocean : and thus the ashes of Wycliffe are the emblem of his doctrine, which now is dispersed all the world over."

12. The followers of Wycliffe were called Lollards, from the German word *lollen*, which means " to sing."   They were so called because of their habit of singing hymns. Wycliffe's " poor priests " went about from place to place, and large crowds gathered to listen to their homely words. The monks and friars were bitterly opposed to them and their followers, and did everything in their power to put them down, but in vain.   The Lollards grew in numbers every day, and about the year 1390 a writer tells us that " every other man you met was a Lollard."

13. Harsh Acts were passed against the Lollards ; but so

strong were they that until Richard the Second had been deposed in favour of his cousin, Henry the Fourth, there was very little persecution. In the year 1401, however, an Act was passed by which Lollards who would not give up their beliefs might be imprisoned and burnt. William Sawtré, the first English martyr, was burnt at Smithfield in the same year. Even this cruel act did not crush the Lollard movement.

14. In the later years of Henry the Fourth's reign the Lollards found a leader in Sir John Oldcastle. Henry died in the year 1413, and was succeeded by his son, Henry the Fifth, the great warrior who made himself master of France. Oldcastle was a great captain and the king's personal friend, but this did not save him from the anger of the clergy. In the year of Henry's accession they tried him as a heretic, found him guilty, and had him sent to the Tower. At this time the Lollards became very active, and a large number of them met in St. Martin's Fields, for the purpose, it was said, of seizing the king. Oldcastle was expected to put himself at their head.

15. Henry showed great promptness ; he led an armed force against them, and dispersed the meeting. Forty of the Lollards were hanged or burnt, and a price was placed on the head of Sir John Oldcastle. In 1417 he was captured, and put to death by being hung in chains over a fire. After the death of Oldcastle the Lollards were no longer a force to be reckoned with ; but they continued to exist, in considerable numbers, in various parts of the country, and especially in London, down to the time when the religion of the people underwent its great change.

SMITHFIELD.

40. "HURLING TIME."—I.

1. To-day we will visit a historic part of London. Starting from St. Paul's Cathedral, we walk down Ludgate Hill, and, turning to the right along Old Bailey, we cross Holborn Viaduct, and pass through Giltspur Street. We now find ourselves in an open space known as Smithfield. In the middle is a railed-in garden with turf and trees and a fountain. On the north side are the extensive buildings containing the London Central Meat Market and the poultry, fish, vegetable, and hay markets, and on the east side is the famous St. Bartholomew's Hospital.

2. In the fourteenth century Smithfield was outside the north-western gate of the city. The name means "smooth field," and in the times of which we are speaking it was the

great jousting ground on which knights were always ready to challenge each other to feats of arms. Giltspur Street reminds us of the same period, for none but knights might wear gilt spurs at their heels.

3. Smithfield has other historic memories too. The Scottish patriot Wallace was beheaded in 1305, near the spot on which we are now standing. Seventy-six years later a deed was done at Smithfield which brought to an end the greatest rising of English labourers known to history.

4. Before I deal with this "Hurling Time," as it is called, let me tell you of a very sad event which happened twenty-eight years before Edward the Third died. In the year 1349 a dreadful plague known as the Black Death ravaged this country. It began in China, where some five millions of persons perished, and slowly spread to the shores of the Black Sea. Brought by sailors to Constantinople, it raged across Europe, and in August 1348 first appeared in these islands at Melcombe Regis in Dorsetshire. Within a fortnight it was in Bristol ; then it reached Gloucester ; and by the beginning of November it was in London. Slowly but surely it spread to all parts of the kingdom.

5. The plague showed itself by large boils and black spots, which were known as " God's tokens." Then followed severe inflammation of the lungs, and death took place often in a few hours, usually in less than three days. The plague attacked all classes, from the daughter of the king to the child of the humblest serf.

6. Thousands of homes were empty ; hundreds of villages were deserted ; the churches were left without clergy, the monasteries without monks, the convents without nuns.

"Sheep and cattle strayed through the fields of corn, and there were none left who could drive them." The harvest was ungathered, the fields were unploughed. "The sound of the grinding was low," and "the mourners went about the streets."

7. In fourteen months the plague was stayed. Let us see what followed. Half the labourers had died, half the fields were untilled, and half the crops lay rotting on the ground. The price of corn was twice what it had been before the plague, and the labourers needed twice their old wages in order to live. Labourers were few, and the land-owners, owing to the death of so many of their tenants, had a great deal of land thrown upon their hands. There were not enough labourers to till the land, and when this happens their wages are sure to rise. For the first time in English history the labourers were able to dictate their own terms to their masters.

8. In some cases the wages asked were more than double what they had been before the plague. Women, for example, who formerly received one penny a day, now demanded twopence and even threepence. Of every quarter of wheat now harvested, one-eighth had to be paid over to the labourer as wages instead of one-twelfth before the plague. The man who threshed the corn also asked one-third more in wages than formerly.

9. In Lesson 33 you learnt that many of the labourers on the manors had won their freedom by payment of a fine to their lords. These free labourers now began to reap a rich harvest. You may be sure that those who were still serfs grew bitterly discontented when they saw the prosperity of

their more fortunate fellows, and longed to be free themselves.

10. The landlords, on the other hand, were being ruined, and in 1349 they persuaded Parliament to pass what is known as the Statute of Labourers. This Act of Parliament began as follows : "A great part of the people, and especially of workmen and servants, having died of the pestilence, many, seeing the necessity of masters and great scarcity of servants, will not serve unless they may receive excessive wages, and some are rather willing to beg in idleness than by labour to get their living."

11. Then the Act went on to say that every labourer, bond or free, able in body and within the age of threescore years, not having land of his own and not in service, should be bound to work for any master who should require him to do so, but that such servants should only receive the wages which were paid in the year before the plague. Any one who refused to work for these wages, or left his work to go elsewhere, was to be sent to jail. If a man asked more than the legal wages, he was to be brought before the court of the manor and made to pay double the wages which he demanded. Similarly, any lord who offered more than the legal wages was to be fined a sum equal to three times what he offered.

12. This law was extremely hard on the labourers. Before the plague the landlords had cared little whether their villeins remained on their manors or left them, so long as they had enough labour to cultivate their demesnes. Those who had left their masters in this way had become free labourers. Now that labour was so scarce and costly, the

masters began to seek out their villeins, and force them to return and do their old service. Lawyers were employed to hunt through the old court rolls for proofs that the so-called free labourers owed services to their lords. Even if a man could show that he was free at the time of Doomsday, it availed him nothing.

13. The labourers became once more bound to the soil, and were not permitted to leave the manor to which they belonged without a pass. Runaway labourers were made outlaws, and when they were captured were branded with the letter **F** to signify their falsity. The town which harboured them was fined ten pounds. These foolish attempts to bring back a state of serfdom which had really passed away were doomed to failure, and you will not be surprised to learn that they made the labourers extremely angry.

14. There were other reasons, too, why the labouring classes should be uneasy and unsettled. The taxes were very high, and, as far as the people could see, the money was wasted by the Government. In many parts of the country the forest laws were very harsh, and led to much angry feeling.

15. In the towns the craftsmen were banded together into gilds, which kept up the price of goods, and the poor labourer was again the victim. Then there was much anger against the Flemings, or people of Flanders, who had been brought over to this country to teach the English cloth-weaving, and by their quickness and skill were able to undersell the native workmen. For these and many other reasons the labourers of England were very discontented, and were ready to revolt.

DEATH OF WAT TILER.

(From the picture by J. Northcote, R.A.)

41. "HURLING TIME."—II.

1. "Hurling Time" began four years after the death of Edward the Third, in the reign of his grandson, Richard the Second. The labourers in many parts of the kingdom had formed clubs for the redress of their grievances. They were encouraged by the old soldiers who had come back from the French wars, and were fond of boasting that the yeoman's arrow could do more than the knight's spear.

2. They were also stirred up by preachers, who went to and fro amongst them throughout the country. A priest named John Ball was a very powerful preacher, and had great influence over the people. One of his sermons was preached on the following text,—

> "When Adam delved and Eve span,
> Who was then the gentleman?"

He said: "Things will never go well in England so long as goods be not in common, and so long as there be villeins and gentlemen. By what right are they whom we call lords greater folk than we are? On what grounds have they deserved it? Why do they hold us as serfs? They have leisure and fine houses; we have pain and labour, the rain and the wind in the fields. And yet it is of us and our toil that these men hold their estate."

3. In May 1381 the labourers were in the condition of dry tinder waiting for a spark to set it ablaze. At that time a tax of twelvepence per head was levied on every person in the kingdom above the age of fourteen. Twelve-pence may not seem a large sum to you, but in those days it

was equivalent to twelve shillings of our present money. In the Kentish town of Maidstone one of the tax collectors insulted the daughter of Wat the Tiler, who gave the signal for the rising to begin by killing the offender with his hammer.

4. The peasantry rose throughout a large part of England. In almost every shire from Somerset to York large numbers of men left their work in the fields, and arming themselves with clubs, rusty swords, axes, old bows, hedge stakes, or anything else they could lay their hands on, marched towards London. There was a good deal of murder and lawlessness on the way, but the rebels, one and all, declared themselves loyal to King Richard.

5. The Essex men under Jack Straw encamped at Hampstead, the Kentish men under Wat the Tiler at Blackheath, and the Hertfordshire folk at Highbury. Then they sent to the boy-king and asked him to speak with them. The king wished to hear what they had to say, but the Archbishop of Canterbury advised him not to " listen to such shoeless rascals."

6. The Lord Mayor of London, William Walworth, and the richer burgesses wished to keep the peasants out of London, but the poorer citizens opened the gates and let their country brethren in. The rebels were especially angry with the lawyers, who had, as they thought, tricked them once more into serfdom. They therefore burnt the Temple and every law book and tax account which they could lay their hands on. They also murdered many Flemings and other aliens.

7. On the fourteenth of July the king rode through

Aldgate out to Mile End Meadow, where he met the Essex men under Jack Straw. Their demands show us the real origin of the movement. "What will ye?" asked the king. "We will," answered the peasants, "that you free us for ever, us and our lands, and that we be never named or held for serfs." "I grant it," said the king, and the Essex men believed him and went quietly home.

8. Meanwhile Wat the Tiler and his followers had broken into the Tower of London, and had beheaded two of the chief officers of the State. This, however, did not frighten the young king, and next morning, with the mayor and several knights, he rode to Smithfield, where we now stand, in order to meet Wat and his host.

9. Tiler rode up on a small horse and dismounted. He held a dagger in one hand, and with the other he shook hands heartily with Richard, and bade him be of good cheer, for he would soon be very popular with the commons. Then Tiler, at the king's request, set forth the demands of the peasants. Richard promised to grant them all.

10. Tiler, remounting his horse, was about to ride away when he overheard one of the knights in the king's train say, "Yonder Tiler is the greatest thief and robber in the county of Kent." Tiler was so angry that he tried to kill the knight with his dagger. Walworth, the Lord Mayor, interfered, and Tiler turned upon him and struck at him. Walworth was saved by his armour, and instantly drew his sword and wounded Tiler in the neck and head. On this one of the royal squires leaped from his horse and stabbed the peasant leader to death as he lay helpless on the ground.

11. At once Wat's friends shouted, "Let us stand together; we will die with our captain, or avenge him. Shoot, lads, shoot!" and they bent their bows. The young king, however, with great coolness and courage, rode towards them and called out, "What is this, my men? Will you shoot your king? Have no care for Wat's death. He was a traitor. I will be your captain; come, follow me, and you shall have the charters which you ask for." Seeing the boldness of the boy, the peasants followed him quietly to Islington, while Walworth rode back into London to gather troops. When the soldiers arrived, the peasants went off quietly to their homes.

12. The rising was at an end; but now that Wat was dead, the knights and rich citizens grew courageous again, and persuaded Richard to break his word. Parliament met in November, and the king said that he had repealed the charters which he had granted, because he had no power to deal with other men's goods or bondsmen. Then came the day of punishment. Thousands of the poor peasants were hanged, and a time of great misery followed.

13. From beginning to end the whole rising lasted only three weeks, nevertheless it marks a very important period in English history. The peasants seemed to have gained nothing, but as a matter of fact they had prevented their masters from setting up again the old slavery. Serfdom was already dead, and it rapidly passed away. As we stand in Smithfield, near the great mcat market where the fat cattle of the shires are sold to feed London's teeming millions, let us remember that here began the freedom which the peasants of England now enjoy.

BOSWORTH FIELD (KING DICK'S WELL).

42. THE WARS OF THE ROSES.

1. To-day we will visit the little town of Market Bosworth, twelve miles to the west of Leicester.   Three miles
to the south-east of Market Bosworth we see what was
formerly a stretch of open uncultivated country known as
Redmore.   It is now enclosed and tilled, and is called
Bosworth Field.   Let us pass on to yonder monument,
which was erected in 1812 over a small spring of water.
The inscription on it tells us that King Richard quenched
his thirst at this spring on the day of the battle of Bosworth
Field.   We are now standing on the scene of the last fight
of the Wars of the Roses.   Here it was that Richard the
Third was slain, and Henry Tudor was crowned King of
England.

2. In Book III. you read an outline of the battles and executions, the treasons and miseries of the long, selfish struggle which is known as the Wars of the Roses. The strife raged, with long intervals of peace, for thirty years, and the chief matter at issue was the rival claim to the throne of the families of York and Lancaster.

3. King Henry the Sixth, the son of the warlike Henry the Fifth, was a frail and feeble man, both in mind and body. He meant well, and was both pious and studious, but he always needed a strong arm to lean upon. In the early part of his reign he found the strong arm in his minister Suffolk ; later in his reign he was ruled by his strong-willed queen, Margaret of Anjou.

4. Now, Suffolk was very unpopular with the English people. The great dominions which Henry the Fifth had won in France were slipping away one by one from the English grasp, and the anger of the people knew no bounds. When at last Normandy and Guienne were lost, and nothing remained save Calais and the Channel Islands, the House of Commons determined to try Suffolk on a charge of high treason. Henry sent his favourite off to Calais so as to be out of the way until the storm blew over. During the voyage Suffolk was captured by some London ships, and, after a mock trial, his head was struck off.

5. Suffolk's friends, however, still remained in power, and Henry would not dismiss them. Discontent was rife everywhere, and in 1450 Jack Cade, a soldier of fortune, raised the Kentish and Sussex men and marched on London. He was easily overcome, but had he been a man of position

and a commander who could have kept his followers in order, the rising might have been very serious indeed.

6. Richard, Duke of York, now came over from Ireland, of which he was governor, and put himself at the head of those who opposed the king. You will remember that Henry the Sixth, who represented the house of Lancaster, was descended from John of Gaunt, Duke of Lancaster, third son of Edward the Third. Richard, Duke of York, was descended, on his mother's side, from Lionel of Clarence, the second son of Edward the Third; and, on his father's side, from Edmund, Duke of York, the fourth son of Edward the Third. He represented the house of York, and through his mother had a better claim to the throne than the man who then occupied it. He expected to be king on the death of Henry, who was childless.

7. York urged Henry to send away Somerset, the minister who had taken the place of Suffolk; but the king refused, and was supported by many of the nobles. Ill-feeling between the parties grew apace. Most of the people of England sided with York, especially the citizens of London and the farmers of the south and the Midlands. In 1453 the king went mad, and York was made Protector of the realm. Just as all the trouble seemed to be past, a son was born to the king, and Henry recovered from his madness. York was at once dismissed, and Somerset took his place.

8. Hastily gathering his retainers and friends, York marched towards London. Somerset and the king met him at St. Albans, and a brief struggle took place in the streets of the old city. Victory rested with York; Somerset was

slain, and the king was captured. This battle marks the beginning of the Wars of the Roses, which you know were so called because the members of the rival parties wore a rose as their badge—a white rose for York, a red rose for Lancaster.

9. When the war broke out, the disbanded soldiers who had fought in France freely offered their services to one side or the other. These hired soldiers, together with the gentry and personal followers of the great nobles, made up the armies which were engaged in the struggle. For the most part the people took little interest in the fighting, and the business of the country was not interrupted. The judges still went on circuits as of old, and the peasant would often pause on his hillside furrow, and lean on the handles of his plough, to view the nobles of the land dashing themselves to pieces in battle on the plain below. The war was a war of a class and not of the nation.

10. Five months after the battle of St. Albans the poor king lost his wits again, and York became Protector a second time. Again, however, the king recovered, and again York was dismissed. Both parties then prepared for war once more. The fierce young Queen Margaret put herself at the head of the king's friends, and journeyed up and down the land enlisting men to wear the "white swan" badge and fight for her infant son's rights.

11. At the head of the nobility stood Richard Neville, Earl of Warwick, afterwards known as the Kingmaker. He was an ambitious man, very rich and very powerful. He had eight hundred followers who wore his badge— "the bear and the ragged staff"—and he was the most

notable person of his day. Some of the queen's retainers tried to murder him, and this led to a fresh outbreak of hostilities.

12. At first the fortune of war rested with the Yorkists. The battle of Northampton, which took place in 1460, resulted in the death of many Lancastrian nobles, the captivity of the king, and the flight of Margaret and her son. York then, for the first time, boldly claimed the throne. Parliament proposed that Henry should remain king for life, and that on his death York should succeed him. To this York agreed.

13. Queen Margaret, however, had to be reckoned with. She hastened north to rouse the Border barons, who hated the Protector. At Wakefield, in the year 1460, she defeated and slew him. His head, crowned in mockery with a diadem of paper, was set up above the gate of York, the " white rose city." So perished the wisest statesman of his time. Richard's place was taken by his son Edward, a warlike young fellow of eighteen, who at once marched on London, and was declared king as Edward the Fourth in the year 1461. Then he set out to defeat his foes and to avenge his father's death.

14. On Palm Sunday, in the same year, the battle of Towton was fought during a storm of wind and snow. The snow drove into the faces of the Lancastrians, and their arrows, blown back by the wind, fell short of the mark. When their quivers were empty, the Yorkists drew near, poured in volley upon volley, and then charged. The Lancastrians fought desperately, but gave way at last, and were pursued and slain without mercy. Thirty thousand men

RICHARD III. AT THE BATTLE OF BOSWORTH.

fell at Towton, and this battle practically decided the war. For several years, however, Margaret, with the aid of the French, kept up a strong resistance in the north. In 1464 she was forced to leave the country.

15. The Yorkist cause now appeared secure, and Edward, who had hitherto acted on Warwick's advice, began to slight him. At last king and Kingmaker quarrelled, and Warwick in bitter anger made a treaty with Margaret, who was then in France. He invaded England on her behalf, and Edward was forced to fly for safety to Holland. Henry was once more placed upon the throne; but six months later Edward returned from exile, raised an army, and slew Warwick at Barnet. A fortnight later he destroyed the remnant of the Lancastrian forces at Tewkesbury.

16. Margaret's son was slain as he fled from the battle, and soon afterwards old King Henry was murdered in the Tower. Thenceforward Edward the Fourth reigned in peace, and when he died in 1483 the crown quietly passed to his son, Edward the Fifth. The long reign of violence and bloodshed, however, was not yet at an end. Richard, Duke of Gloucester, uncle of the boy-king, turned traitor to his nephew, and seized the crown. To secure himself on the throne, he caused young Edward and his brother to be strangled in the Tower.

17. This crime profited him little, for two years later, Henry Tudor, who represented the claim of the Lancastrians, overthrew his forces and slew him at Bosworth Field, where we now stand. Henry was crowned king on the battlefield. Thus the red rose triumphed, and the Wars of the Roses came to an end.

18. What were the results of these years of miserable strife? During the long warfare Yorkist and Lancastrian showed no mercy to each other; they killed and beheaded each other freely, and thus it happened that whole families of nobles passed away. Now, the barons had always been the greatest check on the power of the king, and when their power was gone the kings were able to rule as absolute monarchs. As yet the people had no leaders, and they were glad to be governed by a strong king who could preserve them from the horrors of another civil war. Thus the first result of the wars was to make Henry the Seventh and the other Tudor sovereigns complete masters of the realm.

---

43. THE FIRST ENGLISH PRINTING-PRESS.

1. This morning we will visit St. Margaret's Church, Westminster. It adjoins Westminster Abbey, and is overshadowed by that magnificent pile. St. Margaret's is far less beautiful and far less interesting than Westminster Abbey; nevertheless we shall find our visit to it well repaid.

2. The great interest of the church lies in its memorial windows and monuments. I have brought you to see one of these memorial windows. It is placed at the east end of the south aisle. Look at it. You see that it is to the memory of William Caxton, the first English printer. Caxton's lifework was done in the near neighbourhood, and he lies buried in the church. The window was set up to his memory by the London printers and publishers in the year 1883.

3. Caxton was born in the Weald of Kent, about the year 1422, the year in which Henry the Fifth died.   During his boyhood the French were winning back their country from the English, and when he was thirty-one years of age France was entirely lost to this country. When Caxton was sixteen years of age he went to London, and was bound apprentice to a mercer. After his apprenticeship was over he settled in Bruges, which was then one of the most important business towns on the Continent.   He prospered in his business, and was so highly esteemed that he was made governor of the English merchants who traded in Bruges.

THE CAXTON WINDOW.

4. While Caxton was busy buying and selling cloth in Belgium, the Wars of the Roses broke out.   For thirty years England was the scene of bloodshed and strife.   The rest of Western Europe, however, was at peace, and thousands of earnest men were turning their thoughts towards learning.

Now, men cannot become learned without books. Books are the storehouses of knowledge. They garner the wisdom of past times, so that men can begin learning where their fathers left off. Without books a land can never become really civilized.

5. There were very few books in those days, for every word in them had to be written down by hand. Patient monks laboured day after day in their monasteries copying books, and adorning the initial letters of each chapter with beautiful designs in gold and gay colours. Some of these books took years to complete, and, of course, they were very costly. Only the rich could then afford to possess books.

6. When men turned their thoughts to learning, a demand grew up for more books and cheaper books, and ingenious men were soon busy trying to meet the demand. When Caxton was about twenty-eight years of age, a man named John Gutenberg, living at Mainz, in the valley of the Rhine, made a great discovery. He invented movable types.

7. I dare say you have seen the types which a printer uses. They are small blocks of metal, with their tops shaped like one or other of the letters of the alphabet. The compositor, as the man who "sets up" the type is called, has a large number of these types, which he places side by side to make words. When a page of these types is "set up," the surface is inked, and a piece of paper placed on it and pressed. Each type makes its mark on the paper, and thus we get the words printed.

8. Now, when John Gutenberg in his workshop at

Mainz first made and used movable types, he gave the world one of the greatest boons it has ever received. He enabled thousands of copies of a book to be made in the time formerly occupied in copying one. Thus books could be produced far more cheaply than before. Nowadays printing is so rapidly done that twenty or thirty thousand copies of a large newspaper can easily be printed in an hour. So plentiful and so cheap are books that there is scarcely a home without them. Every one can now buy books, and so every one has a chance of learning.

9. William Caxton was a studious man. He taught himself French, and in his leisure he translated into English the Tales of Troy. People were eager to read these tales, and Caxton naturally wished to have a large number of copies of his book made. He had heard of the new art of printing which was then being carried on at Cologne, and he decided to have his book printed. He went to Cologne and learned the art. Then he returned to Bruges, and set up a press of his own. On this press, in the year 1474, he printed his book. It was the first book ever printed in English. A second book produced in Bruges was "The Game and Playe of the Chesse."

10. Two years later he crossed over to England, carrying his types and his press with him. Edward the Fourth was then King of England, and he showed great favour to Caxton. Edward's brother-in-law, Earl Rivers, was Caxton's intimate friend, and translated for him the first book printed in England. It was called "The Dictes and Sayings of the Philosophers." You may see a copy of this work in the British Museum.

11. Now look at the beautiful picture which forms the frontispiece of this book. It shows you the first printing-office ever established in this country. Notice the arched roof, the carved pillars, and the pointed doorway of the room. It seems to be part of a church building. So it is, for Caxton's press was first set up in one of the buildings belonging to Westminster Abbey. It was known as the Almonry, because it was the place in which the alms were distributed to the poor.

12. People in those days thought that the printers had sold themselves to the Evil One, and that in return for their souls he had taught them the " black art " of printing. The foolish, ignorant Londoners of the time would have smashed Caxton's precious press to matchwood if they could have laid their hands on it. For this reason, Caxton's noble friends enabled him to set up his press in one of the Abbey buildings. Under the shadow of the church he was safe. Notice the monk on the left of the picture. He has crossed his hands on his breast, so as to be safe against the wiles of Satan. He firmly believes that this printing is the work of the Evil One.

13. The king and queen have come to see Caxton at work. They have brought their two little sons and their daughter with them. The eager little princes now looking in wonder at the printing were afterwards murdered in the Tower. Behind, and to the right of the king, stands Richard, Duke of Gloucester, the false uncle who caused them to be put to death.

14. Caxton in his furred gown is working the press, and is pointing out the newly-printed sheet to the king. Look

at the press. It does not differ much from that with which " proofs " are " pulled " nowadays, except that the presses in our composing rooms are made of iron and not of wood.

15. To the right of the press you see a man with two balls made of sheepskin stuffed with wool. With these he dabs the ink on the types. At the bench on the right of the picture you see the compositor. The types are in the " case " in front of him. In his hand is a grooved " stick," which he fills with type to form a line. A somewhat similar " case " and " stick " are in use in our printing-offices to-day. The old man on the other side of the bench is reading a " proof," to see what changes must be made before the page is perfect.

16. To the left of the picture we see a group of four workmen. Two of them are carving wood blocks into letters and designs ; a third is binding the printed sheets into a book. He sews the leaves together in a frame, hammers them to make them flat, covers the back with glue, and fastens on the covers, which are pieces of wood faced with leather and studded with brass nails. The fourth man is painting in bright colours the initial letters of the book.

17. In all, Caxton printed about one hundred books, twenty-four of which he translated himself. When he died, full of years and honour, printing was firmly established in England. We can scarcely overestimate the debt which we owe to this grand old master printer. Had the British people not learnt the art of printing, there would have been neither of those two great blessings upon which we pride ourselves most—our British literature and our British liberty.

18. Our great writers could never have arisen if large numbers of our people had not learned to read, and if the printing-press had not enabled their works to be circulated widely. Our British liberties could never have been won and preserved had men not been able to set forth their rights in print, so that all might know them and stand fast in their defence.

44. LOOKING BACKWARD.

1. When Richard the Third fell dead on Bosworth Field, the golden crown which he had vaingloriously worn on his helmet rolled away and lay hidden beneath a hawthorn bush. Sir William Stanley, to whose treachery Richard's defeat was mainly due, picked it up, and placing it on the victor's head, hailed him as Henry the Seventh, King of England. With this act an important chapter of our history closes and a new one opens. The Middle Ages have passed away, and a new England with a new learning and a new faith is about to dawn.

2. Before we close this book, let us, like wayfarers on a hilltop, pause awhile and look back over the road which we have travelled together. Afar off, we see the Iberian give way to the Celt, and the Celt in turn fall before the legions of Rome. For four long centuries Britain lies under the yoke of the conqueror, and at the end of that time the land bears all the marks of civilization.

3. Unskilled in war and unfamiliar with weapons, the Britons are well-nigh helpless when the stern grip of Rome is relaxed and they are left to defend themselves. They fall

a prey to certain uncivilized tribes of Northern Europe, men fearless of death, and schooled in courage and enterprise by their seafaring life. Britannia becomes England, and the Briton finds a refuge only in the mountains of the west.

4. Then we see these English tribes living in their new land the life of their old home. They set up their townships, their moots, their own system of local government, traces of which still remain among us. In course of time the tribes unite into kingdoms, and the story of our land is mainly the struggle of these kingdoms for mastery. Then comes a mild and softening influence on the rough heathen English. By the zeal of a few Scottish monks and the pious care of Pope Gregory, the people become Christians, and begin to share in the light and learning which the gospel brings.

5. The struggle between the kingdoms still goes on, and there are signs that they will soon be unified under one ruler. Then come the onslaughts of fierce kinsmen still in the heathen stage, and after many years of strife and misery these Danes settle down in the land and even rule it for a time. England becomes one kingdom under one king, and the Danes as years go by become English.

6. Now comes the last successful invasion which our island ever knew. The Normans, the most civilized race of their time, men who also are kinsmen of the English, seize the land and form its ruling class. These Normans set up a new system known as feudalism ; all rights are now connected with the holding of land, and the landless man is nought.

7. The new kings strive to rule on both sides of the

Channel. By doing so they weaken themselves; and as their power wanes, the barons wax in strength. At length they are able to force from the worst of our kings that great statement of national rights known as Magna Charta. In the next reign the foundations of the British Parliament are laid.

8. The ambition of warlike rulers brings about the woeful wars with France, which drag on for a century. The people suffer from heavy taxes; but some good comes out of the evil. The kings become more and more dependent upon their subjects for grants of men and money, and thus the people are the better able to bargain for their freedom.

9. In spite of war, manufactures thrive, trade extends, the towns grow in population, and the great middle class of townsmen becomes important. Then, too, the Great Plague, by reducing the ranks of the labourers, breaks down serfdom, raises wages, and multiplies the number of small landowners and tenant farmers.

10. The terrible Wars of the Roses then begin, and continue for thirty years. The nobles well-nigh perish, and when the wars come to an end the only great check on the power of the king has been removed. The barons have destroyed themselves; the middle classes are not yet strong enough to show their power; and so during the sixteenth century the English sovereigns are absolute masters of the realm. Still, throughout the period with which this book deals, we may see the slow but steady advance of our race. The stormy birth and the hard childhood of the nation are past. The battle of youth and the prosperity of age will fill out the story of later times.

Poetry for Recitation.

1. THE DISCOVERER OF THE NORTH CAPE.

[*The adventurous and daring spirit by which "Britannia rules the waves" is well shown in this account of a voyage of discovery undertaken about 890 A.D. Alfred's character as a truth-teller, patron of arts and sciences, and author, is well brought out in the story told below.*]

1. Othere, the old sea-captain,
   Who dwelt in Helgoland,*
To King Alfred, the Lover of Truth,
Brought a snow-white walrus tooth,
   Which he held in his brown right hand.

2. His figure was tall and stately,
   Like a boy's his eye appeared;
His hair was yellow as hay,
But threads of a silvery gray
   Gleamed in his tawny beard.

3. Hearty and hale was Othere,
   His cheek had the colour of oak;
With a kind of laugh in his speech,
Like the sea-tide on a beach,
   As unto the king he spoke.

---

* Heligoland (Holy Land), a small island in the North Sea, off the mouth of the Elbe, formerly belonging to Britain, now to Germany.

4. And Alfred, King of the Saxons,
　　Had a book upon his knees,
　And wrote down the wondrous tale
　Of him who was first to sail
　　Into the Arctic Seas.

5. " So far I live to the northward,
　　No man lives north of me ;
　To the east are wild mountain-chains,
　And beyond them meres and plains ;
　　To the westward all is sea.

6. " So far I live to the northward,
　　From the harbour of Skeringes-hale,
　If you only sailed by day,
　With a fair wind all the way,.
　　More than a month would you sail.

7. " I own six hundred reindeer,
　　With sheep and swine beside ;
　I have tribute from the Finns—
　Whalebone and reindeer-skins,
　　And ropes of walrus-hide.

8. " I ploughed the land with horses ;
　　But my heart was ill at ease,
　For the old seafaring men
　Came to me now and then,
　　With their sagas * of the seas,—

* Old Norse legends written in poetry.

9." Of Iceland and of Greenland,
 And the stormy Hebrides,
And the undiscovered deep :
I could not eat nor sleep
 For thinking of those seas.

10." To the northward stretched the desert,
 How far I fain would know ;
So at last I sallied forth,
And three days sailed due north,
 As far as the whale-ships go.

11." To the west of me was the ocean,
 To the right the desolate shore ;
But I did not slacken sail
For the walrus or the whale,
 Till after three days more.

12." The days grew longer and longer,
 Till they became as one ;
And southward through the haze
I saw the sullen blaze
 Of the red midnight sun.

13." And then uprose before me,
 Upon the water's edge,
The huge and haggard shape
Of that unknown North Cape,
 Whose form is like a wedge.

14."The sea was rough and stormy,
        The tempest howled and wailed,
    And the sea-fog, like a ghost,
    Haunted that dreary coast;
        But onward still I sailed.

15."Four days I steered to eastward,
        Four days without a night;
    Round in a fiery ring
    Went the great sun, O King,
        With red and lurid light.

*   *   *   *   *

16."And now the land," said Othere,
    " Bent southward suddenly,
    And I followed the curving shore,
    And ever southward bore
        Into a nameless sea.

17."And there we hunted the walrus,
        The narwhale, and the seal;
    Ha! 'twas a noble game!
    And like the lightning's flame
        Flew our harpoons of steel.

18."There were six of us altogether,
        Norsemen of Helgoland;
    In two days and no more
    We killed of them threescore,
        And dragged them to the strand!"

19. Here Alfred, the Truth-teller,
    Suddenly closed his book,
    And lifted his blue eyes,
    With doubt and strange surmise
    Depicted in their look.

20. And Othere, the old sea-captain,
    Stared at him wild and weird ;
    Then smiled, till his shining teeth
    Gleamed white from underneath
    His tawny, quivering beard.

21. And to the King of the Saxons,
    In witness of the truth,
    Raising his noble head,
    He stretched his brown hand, and said,
    " Behold this walrus-tooth ! "

H. W. LONGFELLOW.

2. THE SEA=KING'S GRAVE.

[*This poem breathes in every line the spirit of the old Vikings.*]

1. High over the wild sea-border, on the farthest downs to
       the West,
   Is the green grave-mound of the Norseman, with the
       yew-tree grove on its crest.
   And I heard in the winds his story, as they leapt up salt
       from the wave,
   And tore at the creaking branches that grow from the
       sea-king's grave ;

Some son of the old-world Vikings, the wild sea-wander-
    ing lords,
Who sailed in a snake-prowed galley, with a terror of
    twenty swords.
From the fiords of the sunless winter, they came on an
    icy blast,
Till over the whole world's sea-board the shadow of Odin
    passed,
Till they sped to the inland waters and under the South-
    land skies,
And stared on the puny princes with their blue victorious
    eyes.
And they said he was old and royal, and a warrior all his
    days,
But the king who had slain his brother lived yet in the
    island ways ;
And he came from a hundred battles, and died in his last
    wild quest,
For he said, " I will have my vengeance, and then I will
    take my rest."

2. He had passed on his homeward journey, and the king
    of the isles was dead ;
He had drunken the draught of triumph, and his cup
    was the isle-king's head ;
And he spoke of the song and feasting, and the gladness
    of things to be,
And three days over the waters they rowed on a waveless
    sea ;

Till a small cloud rose to the shoreward, and a gust broke
    out of the cloud,
And the spray beat over the rowers, and the murmur of
    winds was loud
With the voice of the far-off thunders, till the shudder-
    ing air grew warm,
And the day was as dark as at even, and the wild god
    rode on the storm.
But the old man laughed in the thunder as he set his
    casque on his brow,
And he waved his sword in the lightning, and clung to
    the painted prow.
And a shaft from the storm-god's quiver flashed out from
    the flame-flushed skies,
Rang down on his war-worn harness and gleamed in his
    fiery eyes,
And his mail and his crested helmet, and his hair and his
    beard burned red;
And they said, " It is Odin calls ;" and he fell, and they
    found him dead.

3. So here, in his war-guise armoured, they laid him down
    to his rest,
In his casque with the reindeer antlers, and the long
    gray beard on his breast;
His bier was the spoil of the islands, with a sail for a
    shroud beneath,
And an oar of his blood-red galley, and his battle-brand
    in the sheath.

And they buried his bow beside him, and planted the
    grove of yew,
For the grave of a mighty archer, one tree for each of
    his crew,
Where the flowerless cliffs are sheerest, where the sea-
    birds circle and swarm,
And the rocks are at war with the waters, with their
    jagged gray teeth in the storm;
And the huge Atlantic billows sweep in, and the mists
    enclose
The hill with the grass-grown mound where the Norse-
    man's yew-tree grows.

                  RENNELL RODD: *Poems in Many Lands.*

3. THE NORMAN BARON.

[*This poem well illustrates the picture on page* 83, *which shows a Norman
baron on his deathbed giving freedom to his serfs. It is greatly to the credit of the
Church that the monks seized the opportunity—as related in this poem—of securing
the freedom of the down-trodden peasants.*]

   1. In his chamber, weak and dying,
      Was the Norman baron lying;
      Loud without the tempest thundered,
        And the castle-turret shook.

   2. In this fight was Death the gainer,
      Spite of vassal and retainer,
      And the lands his sires had plundered,
        Written in the Doomsday Book.

3. By his bed a monk was seated,
　Who in a humble voice repeated
　Many a prayer and paternoster *
　　From the missal † on his knee.

4. And, amid the tempest pealing,
　Sounds of bells came faintly stealing,
　Bells that, from the neighbouring cloister, ‡
　　Rang for the Nativity. §

5. In the hall the serf and vassal
　Held that night their Christmas wassail ; ‖
　Many a carol, old and saintly,
　　Sang the minstrels and the waits. ¶

6. And so loud these Saxon gleemen
　Sang to slaves the songs of freemen,
　That the storm was heard but faintly
　　Knocking at the castle-gates.

7. Till at length the lays they chanted
　Reached the chamber, terror-haunted,
　Where the monk, with accents holy,
　　Whispered at the baron's ear.

8. Tears upon his eyelids glistened,
　As he paused awhile and listened ;
　And the dying baron slowly
　　Turned his weary head to hear.

---

* Our Father.   † Mass book.   ‡ Monastery.   § Birth of Jesus Christ.
‖ From " Waes hael," meaning " Health to you."   Here used to signify a feast or revel.
¶ Musicians who go about at Christmas time playing Christmas hymns and songs.

9. " Wassail for the kingly Stranger
Born and cradled in a manger !
King like David, Priest like Aaron,
    Christ is born to set us free ! "

10. And the lightning showed the sainted
Figures on the casement painted ;
And exclaimed the shuddering baron,
    " Miserere, Domine ! " *

11. In that hour of deep contrition †
He beheld, with clearer vision,
Through all outward show and fashion,
    Justice the Avenger ‡ rise.

12. All the pomp of earth had vanished,
Falsehood and deceit were banished,
Reason spake more loud than passion,
    And the truth wore no disguise.

13. Every vassal of his banner,
Every serf born to his manor,
All those wronged and wretched creatures,
    By his hand were freed again.

14. And, as on the sacred missal
He recorded their dismissal,
Death relaxed his iron features,
    And the monk replied, " Amen ! "

* " Have mercy, O Lord."   † Grief of heart for sin.
        ‡ One who returns punishment for injury.

15. Many centuries have been numbered
    Since in death the baron slumbered
    By the convent's sculptured portals,
        Mingling with the common dust;

16. But the good deed, through the ages
    Living in historic pages,
    Brighter grows and gleams immortal,
        Unconsumed by moth or rust.

                                    H. W. LONGFELLOW.

4. THE BATTLE OF EVESHAM.

[*This poem describes the battle of Evesham* (1265), *in which Prince Edward, afterwards Edward the First, overcame and slew Simon de Montfort, the great Earl of Leicester, who stood up against the foreigner, and during the two years in which he ruled England, summoned the Parliament which first included lords, borough members, and county members.*]

1. Earl Simon on the Abbey tower
       In summer sunshine stood,
   While helm and lance o'er Greenhill heights
       Come glinting through the wood.
   " My son ! " he cried ; " I know his flag,
       Amongst a thousand glancing ! "
   Fond father, no !—'tis Edward stern,
       In royal strength advancing.

2. The prince fell on him like a hawk,
       At Al'ster yester-eve,*
   And flaunts his captured banner now,
       And flaunts but to deceive.

* Alcester, near Kenilworth, where the younger Simon de Montfort was defeated.

—Look round ! for Mortimer is by,
   And guards the rearward river :—
The hour that parted sire and son
   Has parted them for ever !

3." Young Simon's dead," he thinks, and looked
   Upon his living son ;
 " Now God have mercy on our souls,
   Our bodies are undone !
But, Hugh and Henry, ye can fly,
   Before their bowmen smite us,—
They come on well ! but 'tis from me
   They learned the skill to fight us."

4." For England's cause and England's laws,
   With you we fight and fall !
Together then, and die like men,
   And heaven will hold us all ! "
Then face to face, and limb to limb,
   And sword with sword inwoven,
That stubborn courage of the race
   On Evesham field was proven.

5. O happy hills ! O summer sky,
   Above the valley bent!
Your peacefulness rebukes the rage
   Of blood on blood intent !
No thought was then for death or life,
   Through that long dreadful hour,
While Simon 'mid his faithful few
   Stood like an iron tower,

6. 'Gainst which the winds and waves were hurled
    In vain, unmoved, four square;
And round him stormed the raging swords
    Of Edward and De Clare;
And round him in the narrow combe
    His white-cross comrades rally,
While ghastly gashings cloud the beck
    And crimson all the valley;

7. And triple sword-thrusts meet his sword,
    And thrice the charge he foils,
Though now in threefold flood the foe
    Round those devoted boils.
And still the light of England's cause
    And England's love was o'er him,
Until he saw his gallant boy
    Go down in blood before him!

8. He hove his huge two-handed blade,
    He cried, " 'Tis time to die ! "
And smote about him like a flail
    And cleared a space to lie.
" Thank God ! " he said; nor long could life
    From loved and lost divide him,—
And night fell o'er De Montfort dead,
    And England wept beside him.

F. T. Palgrave.

5. CRÉCY.

[*Edward the Third* (1327–1377 A.D.), *in support of his claim to the French crown, led an army of about* 8,000 *men into France. At the famous battle of Crécy, fought on the banks of the river Somme* (1346 A.D.), *he inflicted a crushing defeat on an army of Frenchmen between* 60,000 *and* 100,000 *in number. The hero of the fight was the youthful Edward the Black Prince. Edward took Calais, and by the year* 1360 *a large part of Southern France was in his hands. Before Edward was in his grave, however, English dominion in France had been reduced to the ports of Bordeaux and Bayonne, with the strip of coast between them, and the fortress of Calais.*]

1. High on a mill-tower Edward stands,
    And scans th' approaching foe;
   He sees King Philip's mailèd bands
   Roll on like waves o'er ocean sands,
    And hears their trumpets blow.

2. The chivalry of France he sees,
    King, prince, duke, viscount, knight,
   Their banners waving in the breeze,
   Their armour gleaming midst the trees—
    A fair and fearsome sight.

3. Their myriad footmen, rank by rank,
    Leap onward to the fray;
   Cross-bowmen swarm on either flank.
   " God, give us all Thy grace to thank
    For victory to-day."

4. King Edward spoke, then turned to view
    His host on Crécy's hill.
   Brave English lads with bows of yew,
   Nought could their valiant souls subdue,
    Nor bend their stubborn will.

5. And foremost midst the English spears
    He sees his gallant son
In knightly guise, a boy in years,
His eyes aflame, as swell the cheers
    That tell the fight's begun.

6. The barbèd shafts like blinding snow
    In deadly flight assail ;
The plain, incarnadined * below,
Is cumbered with the dying foe—
    The living blench and quail.

7. The false cross-bowmen turn and fly
    Beneath that hurricane.
" Charge now for France ! " 'tis Philip's cry.
In fiery whirl his knights reply ;
    The English line they gain.

8. Loud clangs the sword upon the shield ;
    The boy is in the van ;
Bravest of brave on that dread field,
Where stricken princes fall or yield,
    He nobly plays the man.

9. The doubtful conflict rages high ;
    The field runs red with gore ;
Knights to the stalwart Edward hie—
" Help for thy son," they loudly cry ;
    " The foemen press him sore."

* Made red.

10. " What ! is he down ? "   A vision blurs
　　The father's anxious gaze.
　" Nay ?—God be thanked !   No warrior stirs;
　　To-day the boy must win his spurs,
　　The glory his and praise."

11. See! now the foe is backward thrust,
　　The raging fight is o'er,
　The lilied banners * trail the dust,
　King Philip flies, for fly he must,
　　His legions are no more.

12. And Crécy we'll remember long,
　　That field so nobly won,
　And tell our sons in tale and song
　Of England's pride, her archers strong,
　　And Edward's gallant son.

　　　　　　　　　　　　EDWARD SHIRLEY.

6. HENRY THE FIFTH'S SPEECH BEFORE AGINCOURT.

[*Henry the Fifth* (1413–1422), *the most popular king who ever ruled in England, revived Edward the Third's claim to the French crown, and crossed over to France with an army to support his claim. The first event of the war was the successful siege of Harfleur, at the mouth of the Seine (September 1415). From Harfleur Henry marched northward, and after seven days' waiting gave battle to the French with an army of less than 15,000 men to their 50,000. Crécy was close by, and in its turn the village of Agincourt gave its name to a great English victory (October 1415). More than 10,000 French were slain. As at Crécy and Poictiers, the victory was due in great measure to the English archers.*]

Westmoreland.　　　　　Oh that we now had here
But one ten thousand of those men in England
That do no work to-day!

　　　* So called because blazoned with *fleurs-de-lys*.

King Henry.   What's he that wishes so?
My cousin Westmoreland?—No, my fair cousin:
If we are marked to die, we are enow
To do our country loss; and if to live,
The fewer men the greater share of honour.
God's will! I pray thee, wish not one man more:
By Jove, I am not covetous for gold,
Nor care I who doth feed upon my cost;
It yearns me not if men my garments wear;
Such outward things dwell not in my desires:
But if it be a sin to covet honour,
I am the most offending soul alive.
No, faith, my coz,* wish not a man from England:
God's peace! I would not lose so great an honour,
As one man more, methinks, would share from me,
For the best hope I have.   Oh, do not wish one more!
Rather proclaim it, Westmoreland, through my host,
That he which hath no stomach to this fight,
Let him depart; his passport shall be made,
And crowns for convoy † put into his purse:
We would not die in that man's company
That fears his fellowship to die with us.
This day is called the feast of Crispian:
He that outlives this day, and comes safe home,
Will stand a tip-toe when this day is named,
And rouse him at the name of Crispian.
He that outlives this day, and sees old age,
Will yearly on the vigil feast his neighbours,
And say, "To-morrow is St. Crispian;"

---

* Familiar contraction of *cousin.*   † Guard against the difficulties and dangers of the way.

Then will he strip his sleeve and show his scars,
And say, "These wounds I had on Crispin's day."
Old men forget; yet all shall be forgot,
But he'll remember with advantages
What feats he did that day.   Then shall our names,
Familiar in his mouth as household words—
Harry the King, Bedford and Exeter,
Warwick and Talbot, Salisbury and Gloster—
Be in their flowing cups freshly remembered.
This story shall the good man teach his son ;
And Crispin Crispian * shall ne'er go by,
From this day to the ending of the world,
But we in it shall be remembered—
We few, we happy few, we band of brothers ;
For he to-day that sheds his blood with me
Shall be my brother ; be he ne'er so vile,
This day shall gentle his condition ; †
And gentlemen in England, now abed,
Shall think themselves accursed they were not here ;
And hold their manhoods cheap, while any speaks
That fought with us upon St. Crispin's day.

WILLIAM SHAKESPEARE (Henry V., Act iv. Sc. 3).

7. BEFORE BOSWORTH FIELD.

[The Wars of the Roses began with the first battle of St. Albans (1455) and ended with Bosworth Field (1485).   The name was given on account of the badges worn by each house—the Yorkists taking the white rose, and the Lancastrians the red rose.   These wars were the concern mainly of the great nobles, most of whom

---

* Crispinus and Crispianus were brothers, martyred 287 A.D.   They became the patron saints of shoemakers.

† Make himself a gentleman in rank.

were killed in the various battles; the people took little interest in the success of either side. After the battle of Towton, Parliament acknowledged the Yorkist Edward the Fourth as king in place of the Lancastrian Henry the Sixth. On the death of Edward the Fifth, Richard of Gloucester, his brother, became king, but was defeated and slain at Bosworth by Henry Tudor, the Lancastrian representative. Henry married Elizabeth of York, and thus the rival roses were blended.]

1. The winter it is here;
      In woods no small birds sing;
   The forest it is drear,
      But 'twill green again in spring;
   The throstle sweet will sing;—
      Oh, for summer we are fain,
   For the bright suns that will bring
      Our red, red rose again.

2. Round tower and turret sad
      The storm-wind coldly blows,
   But burgh and hall will glad
      When leaves are here for snows.
   And it's oh for merry May,
      And swallows from the main;
   Oh, England will be gay
      When the red rose comes again!

3. There's grief in Clifford's towers;
      There's wail in Warwick's halls;
   No voice in Percy's bowers
      To feast and tourney calls;
   They're far who should bear sway;
      They're banished who should reign:
   But heads for all shall pay
      When the red rose blooms again.

4. O harp, my harp, so long
    That dared not wake thy voice,
Thy time is near for song,
    Thy hour comes to rejoice.
A whisper's in mine ear,
    That to tell to thee I'm fain:
They come who'll free thy fear—
    Our red rose comes again.

WILLIAM COX BENNETT.

SUMMARY OF BRITISH HISTORY,
WITH DATES.

Races of savage men inhabited Britain in very early times. They lived in caves, and hunted wild animals with weapons made of roughly-chipped flints. Succeeding them came a somewhat superior race (the **Iberians,** Lesson 2, page 11), who knew something of carpentry, pottery, and agriculture. These Iberians probably built Stonehenge, that great temple to which the early inhabitants of our islands perhaps gathered to worship the Sun god.

Seven or eight centuries before Christ, the **Celts** (Lesson 2, page 12) crossed over from the Continent and conquered the Iberians. They were tall, blue-eyed, light-haired, fond of fighting, and a much superior race in mind and body to the Iberians. The Celts were divided into many tribes, each with its own prince or chief. Their wealth lay in their herds of cattle. In war they used bronze weapons and chariots. Their priests were called **Druids.** Human sacrifices were common.

These ancient Britons (Lesson 3, pages 14–18) lived in beehive-shaped dwellings, resembling the Zulu kraals of our own day. They lived by herding cattle, farming, and fishing.

B.C.
55. In 55 B.C. the Celts of the British Isles consisted of two great nations—the **Cymry,** in the southern part of Britain, and the **Gaels,** in the Highlands of Scotland and in Ireland.

55. **Julius Cæsar** invaded Britain to punish the Britons for helping their kinsmen in Gaul to oppose the Roman armies. He landed near Romney, in Kent, and beat back the natives ; but not having sufficient troops, he was forced to return to Gaul for the winter.

54. Next year Cæsar returned to Britain with a much larger army. He defeated the Britons under **Cassivelaunus,** and captured Verulam (St. Albans). Having received hostages and promises of tribute, he returned to Gaul.

A.D. No Roman soldier set foot in Britain for nearly a century.

43. The Romans, under the **Emperor Claudius,** began the real conquest of Britain. (Lesson 4, page 21.)

50. **Caractacus,** the British leader, was defeated, and carried a prisoner to Rome. The south-east of Britain was made a Roman province.

A.D.
61.   The **Druids** continually stirred up the people to revolt. The Roman general, Suetonius Paulinus, crossed the Menai Strait to **Mona,** killed all the Druids found there, and destroyed the altars and sacred groves. During his absence the Iceni revolted under Boadicea, their queen. Suetonius hastened back, and defeated the British with great slaughter. Boadicea poisoned herself.

78.   **Julius Agricola** became governor (Lesson 4, page 21), and gradually reduced the whole of Southern Britain. He marched into Scotland, then called Caledonia, and defeated the wild tribes who lived in that country.

81.   Agricola built a **chain of forts** between the Forth and the Clyde to shut out the northern tribes.

84.   Penetrating the Highlands for the last time, he **defeated the Caledonians,** under Galgacus, in Perthshire. Britain south of the Tyne became Roman.

During the next forty years nothing of importance happened. Many of the Roman camps became permanent fortresses, around which towns grew up. To connect these fortresses the Romans made **paved roads,** so that they could march rapidly from fortress to fortress.

121.   The **Emperor Hadrian** visited Britain, and built a **stone wall** between the Tyne and the Solway. (Lesson 4, pages 22–24.)

139.   **Antoninus Pius** built an **earthen wall** between the Forth and the Clyde.

211.   The **Emperor Severus** overcame the Caledonians, strengthened Agricola's wall, and died at York.

During the next two hundred years the Romans remained masters of South Britain.

The **Roman remains** (Lessons 4 and 5, pages 18–30) and the ruins of Roman buildings found in many parts of England afford abundant evidence of the extent and character of the Roman occupation. The British towns became Romanized ; great military roads were made ; better methods of tillage were introduced ; commerce was extended, and the mines were worked. British chiefs wore the Roman dress, spoke Latin, and amused themselves as the Romans did beside the Tiber.

286.   The **Saxons** began to make inroads on the south-east coast ; hence called by the Romans " the Saxon Shore."

306.   Caledonia invaded by bands of rovers from Ireland. These new-comers were known as **Scots.** (Lesson 30, page 156.)

360.   The inroads of the **Scots** and **Picts** began.

410.   Rome was captured by the Goths, and the **Roman emperor ceased to rule** in Britain.

After the departure of the Romans, Britain was left unprotected, and was **constantly attacked** by the Picts and Scots, and later on by the English pirates (Jutes, Saxons, and Angles).

A.D.

449. The Jute chiefs, **Hengist** and **Horsa,** landed on the Isle of Thanet, and conquered Kent.   (Lesson 6, pages 31–33.)

477. The **Saxons** (Lesson 7, page 38) subdued what is now **Sussex,** and later on founded **Wessex.**   They gave their name to Essex, Middlesex, Sussex, and Wessex.

495–
547. The **Angles** (Lesson 8, page 39) conquered the district between the Forth and Thames, and gave their name to the whole country —Angle-land (England), the land of the English.

These newcomers were uncivilized **heathens.**   (Lesson 9, pages 43–47.)   In this hopeless belief the English remained for nearly one hundred and fifty years after their first invasion.

The English gained a great victory at **Deorham,** in Gloucestershire, and won for themselves the plain of the Severn.

597. Pope Gregory sent Augustine and a band of missionaries to convert the English to **Christianity.**   (Lesson 9, page 46.)

Ethelbert, King of Kent, was converted, and Augustine became first Archbishop of Canterbury.   Gradually the rest of England became Christian.   In 563 **Columba** had founded a monastery on the island of Iona, and began to convert the western part of Scotland.   (Lesson 30, page 156.)

In the year 566 a royal lady named **Hilda** founded an abbey for monks and nuns at Whitby.   In this abbey the **first great English song** (Lesson 10, pages 49–54) was composed.   The composer was **Cædmon.**

613. The Welsh defeated at **Chester,** and Strathclyde cut off from Wales. (Lesson 28, page 146.)

626. **Edwin,** King of Northumbria, became overlord of England.

670. Edinburgh was founded by Edwin of Northumbria, and became the capital of the Northumbrian kingdom.   (Lesson 30, page 157.)

784. **Offa** of Mercia subdued Northumbria and Wessex, and became very powerful.   (Lesson 8, page 42.)

802. **Egbert,** King of Wessex, defeated the Mercians, and became Overlord of England.

The **Vikings** (Lessons 15 and 16, pages 72-80), or Northmen from the coasts of Denmark, Sweden, and Norway, had been raiding the coasts of England for the past sixty years.   Egbert tried hard to beat them off, but after his death his successors were unable to do so.

839–
855. The Danes wintered in the **Isle of Sheppey,** and began to settle in the country.

A.D.	
847.	Kenneth MacAlpin, a prince of Dalriada, united Caledonia under one sovereign. It was then named Scotland. (Lesson 31, page 58.)
849.	**Alfred the Great** (Lessons 13 and 14, pages 65–72), fourth son of King Ethelwulf, was born.
858.	Death of King **Ethelwulf**. **Ethelbald** his son became king of Kent and Sussex. (Lesson 13, page 66.)
861.	Ethelbald died. His brother **Ethelbert** became king of the reunited kingdom. (Lesson 13, page 67.)
866.	Ethelbert reigned five years. **Ethelred**, the third son of King Ethelwulf, became king, and Alfred, his brother, now in his eighteenth year, ruled with him. (Lesson 13, page 67.)
871.	Death of Ethelred. **Alfred the Great became king,** and opposed the Danes (Lesson 14, page 68), who gained possession of the whole of the eastern side of the **Danelaw,** the country as far south as the Thames.
878.	Fresh swarms of **Danes** continually arrived, and London and Winchester were seized. Alfred was forced to seek refuge in the marshes of Athelney (Somersetshire). (Lesson 14, page 68.)
879.	Alfred defeated the Danes at **Ethandun,** and peace was made with their leader, Guthrum, at Wedmore. By this treaty the Danes were to hold the lands of the East Angles and the East Saxons, and to become Christians. Alfred then began to strengthen his kingdom and improve the lot of his people. He built a fleet of warships, and put the "fyrd" or national militia on a better footing. He drew up a code of laws from the old laws of Wessex, reformed the Church, and encouraged education. There are few other names in history to compare with his. (Lesson 14, pages 70–72.)
901.	**Alfred died** at the age of fifty-two.
925.	**Edward the Elder** succeeded Alfred, and defeated the Danes.
937.	King **Athelstan,** Edward's son, fought a great battle against the Vikings and the Scots, and won a splendid victory at **Brunanburgh** (Lesson 16, page 77), after which he had little trouble from either Scot or Northman.
940.	In the reign of **Edmund,** brother of Athelstan, the whole **Danelaw** south of the Humber was **recovered** from the Danes. (Lesson 16, page 77.)
959.	**Edgar the Peace-winner,** brother of Edwy, was the first real King of all England. (Lesson 16, page 77.)
978.	**Ethelred the Redeless,** or Ill-counselled, was set upon the throne. Then came a time of grave danger. The raids of the Vikings began again. (Lesson 16, page 78.) Ethelred bought a truce with the

A.D.	
	Danes, and raised money for buying off the invaders by a tax called **Danegeld.**
1002.	On **St. Brice's Day** a massacre of the Danes in England took place by the king's order.
1003.	**Sweyn,** King of Denmark, invaded England to revenge the massacre. After ten years of fighting, Ethelred was forced to flee to
1013.	Normandy, and the Witan chose Sweyn as king in his stead.
1010.	Llywelyn became chief king of Wales. (Lesson 28, page 147.)
1016.	**Canute** or **Cnut,** Sweyn's son, succeeded his father and carried on the war. He was also king of Norway and Denmark. England has had few better rulers than Cnut. He restored many of the best laws of the old kings, and placed Englishmen in all the important offices. (Lesson 16, page 79.)
1035.	On his death one of Cnut's sons became king of Norway, and the other, named Harold, king of England. Both were dead in seven years, and then **Edward the Confessor,** son of Ethelred the
1042.	Redeless, became king. He had been brought up in Normandy (Lesson 35, page 178), and he filled his court with foreigners.
1049.	Edward the Confessor began to build Westminster Abbey.
1051.	**Godwin,** Earl of Kent, the champion of Englishmen against the foreigner, was forced to seek shelter in Flanders. The burghers of Dover had attacked Eustace, Count of Boulogne, who had married the king's sister. The king ordered Godwin to punish them. Godwin refused, and withdrew beyond the seas.
1051.	**William, Duke of Normandy,** visited Edward in England, and was promised the crown.
1052.	Godwin was recalled, and the Norman favourites were outlawed. Godwin died soon after, and was succeeded by his son Harold.
1060.	**Harold** was **wrecked** on the coast of Normandy. Duke William seized him, but released him on his swearing to support William's claim to the English crown.
1066.	On the death of Edward the Confessor, **Harold** was **elected king** by the Witan.
	Harald Hardrada, King of Norway, and Tostig, brother of Harold, invaded Northumbria, and were defeated by Harold at **Stamford Bridge,** Yorkshire (September 25).
	William of Normandy landed at Pevensey in Sussex (September 28). Harold marched southward, and was defeated and slain in the **Battle of Senlac** (or Hastings), October 14.
	The Witan met at London, and chose **Edgar the Ætheling,** grandson of Edmund Ironside, as king.

A.D.
1066.   **William** threatened London, and Archbishop Stigand offered him the crown.   He was **crowned at Westminster** on Christmas day.

1067.   William visited Normandy.   The tyranny of his regents excited revolts of the English.

1069.   A great rising took place in the north, which was joined by the Welsh, Scots, and Danes.   It was crushed by William, who wasted Yorkshire from the Humber to the Tees.

1070.   Stigand was deposed, and Lanfranc summoned from Normandy to take his place.   Thereafter the English prelates and abbots were generally set aside for Normans all over England.

1071.   William forced the last stronghold of the English in the Fens of Ely, but **Hereward the Wake,** their leader, escaped.   This was the last rising of the English.   The Norman Conquest was now complete.

1072.   William marched into Scotland and received the **submission of Malcolm the Third.**   (Lesson 31, page 159).

William introduced a new system of land-holding called the **Feudal System,** and forced every landholder in the kingdom to do him homage in person at the **Salisbury Moot.**

1078.   The oldest part of the Tower of London, the **White Tower,** was built by William the Conqueror.   (Lesson 19, page 93.)

1079.   William besieged his son Robert in the Castle of Gerberoi (Normandy).   They met in single combat, and the king was unhorsed and wounded.

1081.   William invaded Wales, seized Cardiff, and built its castle.

1085–1087.   The **Doomsday Book** (Lesson 18, pages 89–93) was compiled by William's order.

1087.   **William died** from the effects of an accident, at Mantes, in France.

In this reign **forest laws** were passed, imposing severe penalties on those who injured game in the royal estates.

By the Normans also the custom was instituted of ringing the **curfew bell** every night at eight o'clock, as a signal for all fires and candles to be put out.

1087.   The Norman barons plotted to place Robert (the Conqueror's eldest son) on the throne.   The English supported William Rufus, or the Red (the second son), who was crowned king.

1091.   William attempted to take Normandy from Robert.   It was agreed that the survivor should hold the united dominions.

1095.
1097.   The **First Crusade** was preached by Peter the Hermit.   In order to join it, Robert of Normandy sold his dukedom to William.

1100.   **William the Red** was found **dead** in the New Forest, with an arrow in his breast.

A.D.	
1100.	Robert being absent on the Crusade, **Henry the First** (the Scholar), the third son of the Conqueror, seized the throne. He married Edith-Matilda, daughter of Malcolm the Third of Scotland, and of Margaret, sister of Edgar the Ætheling.
1106.	Henry **invaded Normandy,** and defeated his brother Robert, who was taken prisoner. He was confined in Cardiff Castle till his death in 1135.
1114.	The king's daughter, Matilda or Maud, was married to the Emperor Henry the Fifth of Germany.
1120.	The king's only son, William, was drowned in the wreck of the **White Ship** in the English Channel.
1124.	David the First of Scotland began to reign. He was one of the most renowned of Scottish kings. (Lesson 31, pages 160, 161.)
1126.	Henry required his barons to promise to accept the Empress Matilda as his successor.
1128.	The Emperor, Henry the Fifth, having died, Matilda married Geoffrey, Count of Anjou, a boy of sixteen.
1135.	Henry the First died, leaving his daughter Matilda as his heir.
	Many of the English barons objected to being ruled by a woman. They preferred **Stephen** (son of the Conqueror's daughter), and he was crowned at Westminster. His election was due mainly to the promises he made to all classes—especially to the barons, whom he allowed to **build castles** (Lesson 19, page 99) on their estates.
1136.	The Welsh, under Griffith ap Rees, defeated the English at Cardigan. (Lesson 29, page 149.)
1138.	King **David of Scotland,** Matilda's uncle, invaded England in support of her claim to the throne. He was defeated at **Northallerton** (Yorkshire), in the Battle of the Standard. (Lesson 31, page 160.)
1139.	**War** raged between the supporters of Stephen and those of Matilda, who landed on the south coast with 140 knights. (Lesson 21, page 99.)
1141.	**Stephen** was taken **prisoner** at the Battle of Lincoln, and Matilda acknowledged as queen. Her half-brother Robert was captured, and exchanged for Stephen.
1147.	Matilda withdraws to Normandy.
1152.	Matilda's son, **Henry, landed** in England, and claimed the throne.
1153.	**A treaty** was made between Henry and Stephen at **Wallingford,**
1154.	by which Henry was to succeed Stephen.
	Stephen died. It was in Stephen's reign that **tournaments** (Lesson 20, pages 100–104) were first held in England.
	Henry the Second came to the throne, and set about restoring

A.D.

which, besides barons, prelates, and knights of the shire, he summoned representatives from **cities and boroughs.** This was the beginning of Parliament in its modern form.

Prince Edward, having escaped, defeated Earl Simon at **Evesham** (Worcestershire). Earl Simon was killed, and King Henry was released. (Lesson 26, page 137.)

1272.   **Henry the Third died. Edward the First,** his son, came to the throne.

1274.   Llywelyn refused to do homage. (Lesson 29, page 151.)

1282.   **Llywelyn,** Prince of Wales, was slain, and Wales was subdued. Six months later his brother David was captured and executed. (Lesson 29, page 151.)

1284.   Prince Edward was born at Carnarvon, and was the first English **Prince of Wales. Statute of Wales** passed at Rhuddlan. (Lesson 29, page 151.)

1286.   Alexander the Third of Scotland was accidentally killed, and his infant grand-daughter, the Maid of Norway, became heiress to the crown. (Lesson 32, page 163.)

1290.   The Maid of Norway died. Scotland was ruled by regents for four years. (Lesson 32, page 163.)

1291.   Edward the First of England agreed to decide between the candidates for the Scottish crown, if his overlordship was acknowledged. He chose **John Baliol** as king. (Lesson 32, page 164.)

1296.   Edward, provoked by Baliol's defiance of him, ravaged Scotland, deposed Baliol, and made the Earl of Surrey guardian or governor of the country. (Lesson 32, page 164.)

1297.   The Scots rose under **William Wallace,** who defeated the English forces at Stirling. (Lesson 32, page 165.)

1298.   At **Falkirk,** Wallace was overthrown by Edward. (Lesson 32, page 165.)

1305.   **Stirling Castle surrendered** to Edward, who thought that Scotland was now quite subdued.

1306.   The Scots again revolted under **Robert Bruce,** who was crowned at Scone. (Lesson 32, page 165.)

1307.   Bruce defeated Pembroke at **Loudon Hill** (Ayrshire), and his revolt made rapid progress.

Edward marched against Bruce, reached Cumberland, and **died** at Burgh-on-Sands, near Carlisle. His son, **Edward the Second,** succeeded to the throne. (Lesson 32, page 166.)

1314.   Bruce defeated the English at **Bannockburn,** and made Scotland free. (Lesson 32, page 166.)

A.D.
1327. Parliament (at Westminster) **deposed Edward the Second,** and proclaimed his son king, as Edward the Third.

Nothing is really known of the death of Edward the Second, but he is believed to have been murdered with great cruelty in Berkeley Castle (Gloucestershire), in September 1327.

1328. By the Treaty of Northampton, the **independence of Scotland** was confirmed.

1337. Edward **claimed the crown of France** in right of his mother Isabella. (Lesson 35, page 178.)

1340. The **French fleet was destroyed** off Sluys. (Lesson 35, page 180.)

1346. Edward **invaded France,** landing at La Hogue. He gained a great victory at **Crécy,** and laid siege to Calais. (Lesson 34, page 175.)

1347. Calais surrendered to Edward after a year's siege. (Lesson 36, page 182.)

1349. The **Black Death** carried off nearly one-third of the English people. (Lesson 40, page 200.)

1356. The **Black Prince,** eldest son of Edward the Third, won a great victory over the French at **Poictiers.** (Lesson 36, page 182.)

1360. The **Treaty of Bretigny** was concluded between England and France. (Lesson 36, page 183.)

1376. The **Black Prince died.**

1377. **Edward the Third died,** and was succeeded by **Richard the Second,** son of Edward the Black Prince.

1381. **"Hurling Time."** The peasants of England revolted. Wat Tiler, the Kentish leader, was slain. The revolt, in which many thousands perished, seemed to have failed, but actually it meant the end of serfdom. (Lesson 40, pages 199–203.)

1397. Richard the Second banished Henry of Bolingbroke, Duke of Hereford, and son of John of Gaunt.

1399. During Richard's absence in Ireland, Hereford returned to claim the estates of his father, who had died. His friends flocked to his standard. **Richard was deposed,** and Hereford was proclaimed as **Henry the Fourth.** He was the grandson of Edward the Third.

1400. Richard, the deposed king, died in Pontefract Castle.

1413. Henry the Fourth died, and was succeeded by his son, **Henry the Fifth,** who resumed the war with France. (Lesson 36, page 185.)

1415. Henry claimed the provinces assigned to the king of England by the Treaty of Bretigny (1360), invaded France, took Harfleur, and defeated the French at **Agincourt.** (Lesson 36, page 185.)

1417. Normandy was conquered, and Henry became master of the greater part of France.

A.D.
1420. By the **Treaty of Troyes** it was arranged that Henry should be king of France after the death of Charles the Sixth, and regent until that time. (Lesson 36, page 186.)

1422. **Henry died,** and as his son was a baby a Council of Regency was appointed, with the Duke of Gloucester as Protector. The Duke of Bedford was regent of France. **Caxton** born. (Lesson 43, page 217.)

1429. The siege of Orleans was raised by **Joan of Arc,** and Charles the Seventh was crowned at Rheims. (Lesson 36, page 187.)

1435. **Bedford died,** and the English power in France slowly passed away. (Lesson 36, page 187.)

1445. Henry married Margaret of Anjou. (Lesson 42, page 210.)

1450. The men of Kent rose in revolt under **Jack Cade.** (Lesson 42, page 210.)

1451. The French recovered all the English territories in France except the town of Calais. (Lesson 42, page 211.)

1453. The king was seized with a fit of insanity, and **Richard, Duke of York,** was made Protector. (Lesson 42, page 211.)

1455. Henry recovered. York was dismissed, and Somerset restored to power. York appealed to arms, and the **Wars of the Roses** began. The Yorkists won a victory at **St. Albans.** (Lesson 42, page 211.)

1461. The Yorkists were victorious too at **Northampton,** and York was declared Henry's heir. (Lesson 42, page 213.)

York was defeated and slain at **Wakefield.** (Lesson 42, page 213.)

1461. His son Edward was declared king as **Edward the Fourth.**

1470. The **Earl of Warwick** (the "King-Maker"), who had been chiefly instrumental in making Edward the Fourth king, and with whom he had quarrelled, now joined Margaret, and **restored Henry** to the throne. Edward fled abroad for safety. (Lesson 42, pages 212, 215.)

1471. Edward returned; he defeated and slew Warwick at **Barnet.** A fortnight later he defeated Margaret and killed her son at **Tewkesbury.** (Lesson 42, page 215.)

1476. The **first book was printed** in England by Caxton. (Lesson 43, page 216.)

1483. Edward the Fourth died, and was succeeded by his son Edward the Fifth. **Richard, Duke of Gloucester,** was proclaimed Protector. Edward and his brother were murdered in the Tower, and Gloucester declared himself **king.** (Lesson 42, page 215.)

1485. Henry Tudor, descended, on his mother's side, from John Beaufort, third son of John of Gaunt (third son of Edward the Third), defeated and slew Richard at **Bosworth Field.** **Henry** proclaimed **king.** (Lesson 42, page 215.)